A Life with Horses

D1568612

OTHER TITLES BY MARK

Big Horses, Good Dogs, and Straight Fences:
Musings of Everyday Ranch Life

Horsemanship Through Life

Life Lessons from a Ranch Horse

Horses Never Lie

A Good Horse Is Never a Bad Color

Considering the Horse

OTHER TITLES BY KATHLEEN

In the Company of Horses:
A Year on the Road with Horseman Mark Rashid

A Life with

Horses

Spirit of The Work

Mark Rashid &

Kathleen Lindley

JOHNSON BOOKS

Boulder

THIS BOOK IS DEDICATED TO

all the kind folks who have allowed

us to practice our craft while

helping them with their horses.

—Mark and Kathleen

Published by Johnson Books, a Big Earth Publishing company,
3005 Center Green Drive, Suite 220, Boulder, Colorado 80301.
E-mail: books@bigearthpublishing.com
www.bigearthpublishing.com
1-800-258-5830

Cover and text design by Rebecca Finkel

9   8   7   6   5   4   3   2   1

Library of Congress Cataloging-in-Publication Data
Rashid, Mark.
   Life with horses: spirit of the work / Mark Rashid &
Kathleen Lindley.
      p.   cm.
   ISBN 978-1-55566-407-7
   1. Horses—Training. 2. Horses—Behavior. 3. Horses—
Psychology. I. Lindley, Kathleen.
II. Title.
   SF287.R287   2007
   636.1'088—dc22
                                    2007019306

Printed in China

CONTENTS

Introduction

THIS BOOK HAD ITS BEGINNINGS with the desire to give a small heartfelt gift to a friend. I set out to take some photos of Mark Rashid and his buddy Tim Harvey working with Tim's horse, Tico, at a clinic down in Florida. Since I already had my camera out, I took other pictures while I was at it.

Mark and I have known each other since 1995, when I took a horse I was having trouble with to one of his clinics. I was quite taken with the work he was doing with people and their horses, and I became a regular student. In late 2004, I began traveling with him as his full-time assistant. We've traveled more than 100,000 miles together, and, in the process, I've gained an intimate knowledge of what Mark has simply called "The Work."

The Work is what we do and what is shown in the following pictures. It has a life of its own, but it lives through the people who practice it. Mark learned The Work from Walter Pruitt, "the old man" spoken of in Mark's many books. We don't really know who Walter learned it from, so the family tree, if we think of it that way, starts with Walter. Walter passed The Work to Mark, and Mark has passed it to me and others. When I told Mark that I wasn't sure I was the one to talk about what The Work is in the introduction for this book, he simply said, "The Work is yours now, too."

Being a part of the family tree of The Work is a huge responsibility because, first and foremost, The Work must retain its integrity. When Mark first spoke to me about The Work and my part in it years ago, I thought of it as techniques and things we did with the horses and riders we worked with at clinics. But what I discovered, as I immersed myself in The Work, was that it is not just things we do with horses. It's a way to be, a way to go, a life led a certain way. In order for The Work to be The Work, in order for it to have integrity, it must go all the way through and become who we are.

Because I began shooting these pictures as a gift, I think I put a little different part of myself into them than I had put into any other photos I'd taken, plus I never intended anyone but Tim, Mark, and myself to see them. The first look I got at the photos was when Mark and I were driving out of Florida heading for home in Colorado, and I downloaded them onto my computer. I'd only seen half a dozen of them when I told Mark that I thought something special might have happened. He looked at them and agreed and about thirty minutes later voiced the idea of putting this book together.

I took about a thousand photographs over a two-month period. They were taken on our trips to Georgia, Florida, and California in the winter of 2006. The text was written while we were working the California clinics, where Mark often arose by 5 A.M. to write for several hours before starting his clinic work for the day. Many portions were written while both of us worked side by side on our computers before and after clinicing as well. Some portions were even written in the cab of the truck between California and Colorado. With the vast majority of the photos in the book, you will find that Mark and I have both commented on what was going on at the time the photo was taken. However, we also found very early on in the writing process that for some of the pictures it was sufficient for just one of us to comment, and for others it was not necessary for either of us to comment because we felt the photos spoke for themselves.

It didn't occur to me until we were finishing up this project that although these photos started as a gift for our friend Tim, they became an unexpected gift to Mark and myself as well. My apprenticeship with Mark ended at the close of 2006, and since we now each have our own separate clinic schedules, we don't know how often we'll be able to work together in the future. But through this project, we received the gift of more time to do what we enjoy—working side by side in *A Life with Horses*.

—K.L.

Hands

I AM A FIRM BELIEVER that the best horse training tools ever known to mankind are not ones that can be bought and paid for. Rather they are things we all carry with us everyday, all day … simply put, they are the human mind and body. When working properly, these tools can help establish a relationship between a horse and human that can supercede anything we have experienced before. In fact, these tools can be so powerful that (being restrained only by the bounds of reality), if the mind can imagine it … with practice, the body can perform it.

The key to making a connection with a horse using the human mind and body is our ability to transfer information efficiently from the human to the horse and then receive information back. In the vast majority of cases, the conduit for this transfer is through the human hands, whether those hands are on the reins, a lead rope, or simply being used to pet the horse for a job well done.

The human hand, in and of itself, is an amazing tool. It has the ability to be soft as a feather, then a split second later be hard as iron. It can break a brick or soothe a baby. It can be the instrument of death and destruction or be extended in friendship and hope. When it comes to our work with horses, it can either be used to frighten and worry, or calm and encourage. My belief is, most of all, when it comes to working with horses that the human hand can and should become a tool for the development of mutual trust and understanding.

—M.R.

Kathleen *A horseman's life is in his hands, really. His hands are essential to his trade, and through them he both gathers information and disseminates information. Photographically, I found myself shooting hands constantly, and then pouring over the photos to see what kind of story they told. It seemed to me that the photos of hands had a lot of information and feeling packed into them, even though they were of a fairly "simple" subject. I've heard Mark say that softness doesn't come from one's hands, it comes from one's heart. If that's true, then a picture of a horseman's hands at work is actually a picture of his heart.*

In a clinic setting, we sometimes see horses who have anywhere from mild to profound physical issues that are at the root of what might appear to be training or "attitude" problems. One of the ways we can evaluate these horses is to put our hands on them, to feel joints and muscles, movement or lack of movement, and to look for behavioral changes associated with being touched. We can gather quite a bit of information by watching the horse move, but there is some information we can only gather through actually touching the horse.

In this photo, Mark is examining a horse that came to a clinic in California because he was displaying some behavioral problems. When Mark heard the owner's description of the horse's issues, he asked if he could examine the horse. This photo shows Mark doing his initial examination of the horse's girth area. He's using his hands to gather information. He could be feeling the texture of the tissues under his fingers or the shapes of the bones and cartilage. After he gathered that information, he began pressing gently on the horse's ribs and sternum to see what his response would be. Just a bit of pressure from Mark's hand caused this horse to raise his head, wring his tail, and move away from Mark—a pretty positive pain response.

Mark One of the problems this horse had was that he was cinchy. In other words, any time someone went to tighten his cinch, he would get very agitated, pin his ears, swish his tail, stomp his feet, and sometimes even try to bite. Along with the horse showing signs of being cinchy, the owner also mentioned he would often get very worried and would try to rush or get "jiggy" when coming home from a trail ride. He also had trouble performing smooth transitions.

Normally, folks who have horses with these types of issues automatically assume the issues are specifically related in some way to training, and sometimes they are. But more often than not, these types of issues have very little to do with training, and have everything to do with some kind of physical ailment the horse has developed, or perhaps a problem with ill-fitting tack, or in some cases—both.

After hearing about the symptoms this horse was exhibiting, I decided before we tried to remedy the issues through training, we might first check to make sure there weren't any physical problems. This photo was taken as I was checking to see if the horse would react in any way if I gently palpated his girth area with my hand. I am on his left side, and almost as soon as I touched him, he raised his head, pinned his ears, wrung his tail, and snapped his teeth. A second gentle palpation received almost the same reaction.

The part of the horse's body where my hand is, is an area often overlooked when thinking about the possibility of physical issues in horses. Yet, a simple examination of the area can often tell volumes about whether or not a horse is reacting badly due to something being physically wrong with him, or because there are other issues at hand.

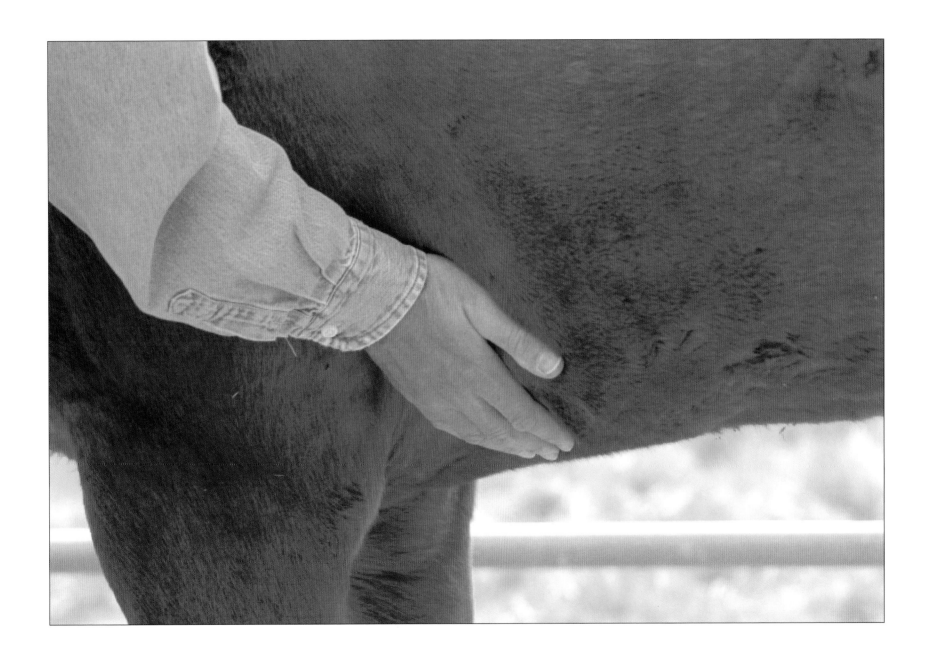

Kathleen *Here, Mark is continuing his evaluation of the horse. Mark is on his right side now, and rather than taking a photo of Mark's examination, I wanted to look at the horse's response to being touched in his girth area. This horse is clearly worried, and Mark has his free hand on the horse's halter to give the horse some guidance if he feels he needs to bite. This horse was worried about anyone touching his girth area, and I could imagine that he would be quite defensive about being cinched up. Through this physical examination, we were able to put a reason behind some of this horse's troublesome behavior. Owners are often relieved to discover that their horse has a physical issue that is hampering their training progress. After all, that means they're probably training the horse just fine, and once the physical issue is resolved, the training they're doing may well be more effective and successful.*

Mark The horse has offered to bite on a couple of occasions when we were taking a look at his left side, so as a precaution, I have taken hold of his halter while I check the right side. I am not trying to stop the horse from giving me feedback about what he's feeling, but rather keeping contact with him so if he feels the need to defend himself, I can direct him without anyone getting hurt.

At this point, we already know he has a physical problem in his girth area. All I'm doing now is trying to assess the extent of it. In other words, is he only sore on his left side, or is the right side also sore and inflamed, which after just a short check of the area, proved it was.

In this photo, it is clear the horse is more worried than he is mad, and shortly after this photo was taken we left him alone and consulted both a vet and an equine chiropractor. Within a couple of days with care from both, the owner was riding him again, and she told us he was the softest she had ever felt him go.

Kathleen *Here's our cinchy bay horse again, except now he's being treated by equine chiropractor Dr. Dave Siemens. I really like how soft this horse looks here compared to the worry we saw in the previous photo. I've seen Dr. Dave work on a lot of horses, and in so many of them, we can see the relief they experience knowing that help is on the way. In this horse's case, he was very easy for Dave to work with, and after being adjusted, his owner was able to ride him successfully.*

Dr. Dave is another horseman who makes his living with his hands. He told me once that in chiropractic school he and his fellow students would take a human hair and put it between the pages of Gray's Anatomy *and have contests to see who could feel the hair with the most pages laid over it. Few of us practice using our hands that way, so it's not much of a surprise that Dave can sometimes feel things others can't.*

Mark Dave and I have known each other for more than twenty years, and much of what I know about equine anatomy and biomechanics I have learned from him. We have spent countless hours together discussing movement in horses, saddle fit, foot and teeth care, muscle, ligament and tendon function and placement, along with training issues and techniques that might be affected by the various physical afflictions horses often suffer from. These days Dave and I have taken to traveling together whenever possible, so if and when we run into physical issues with horses during clinics, he is there to help give them some relief.

The adjustments Dave makes have a lot to do with what he feels through his hands. He can evaluate the amount of movement, or lack thereof, in a specific joint, allowing that joint to move as far as it can on its own, then helping it move just a little more to ultimately help restore full range of motion in the joint. It takes years of practice to achieve the kind of sensitivity Dave exhibits through the use of his hands, and thousands of horses all over the world, this one included, have benefited from his expertise.

Kathleen *Ground-driving was something I'd never heard of before I began working with Mark. Of course, I'd seen people drive horses with vehicles hitched to them, but I'd never seen anyone drive a horse from the ground. I saw Mark use ground-driving as a step in his colt-starting process, after lunging and before riding, to teach a horse to stop, back up, go, and turn softly before stepping on board. That made a lot of sense to me. I've also seen Mark use ground-driving in other situations with saddle horses when there's a specific issue going on that can be addressed through driving.*

When one is ground-driving, the lines are in constant motion, being gathered and slipped, gathered and slipped. One hand may gather while the other slips. Both hands may gather. It was this interplay of movement that I was watching the day I took this photo of Mark ground-driving a Mustang in Florida. Mark's doing something different with each line; we can see that from the quality of the feel in each rope and that he's holding each rope differently. What's interesting is that considering how much is going on here with the ropes, there's a calmness and peacefulness. Mark's done this before and it shows.

Mark I began ground-driving horses as part of their initial starting process years ago when I was a kid. From there I took to driving horses in buggies and carts and ultimately ended up driving Draft horses while pulling wagons, plows, and other farm implements. At one point I was even driving four- and six-up hitches of Draft horses.

One would think you wouldn't be able to feel much from a team of horses by being so far away from them and by only being physically connected to them by leather lines that can be twenty, forty, and sometimes even sixty or eighty feet long. But actually, there is a tremendous amount of information being passed back and forth through those lines at any given time.

It's the same with ground-driving. I use two 32-foot cotton ropes, braided into lines for the work I do. I like the feel of cotton rather than the feel of a synthetic rope or even the flat driving lines you can buy. The flat lines have very little life to them, and the synthetic lines feel … well … synthetic. There is the slightest little give in the cotton lines, which I like. They're forgiving, somehow, both to the horse and to the handler. When things are working just right, and both the horse and I are soft and in tune with one another, there is a sort of dance that happens between the fingers of my hands and the horse's body and feet. Now, one can obviously get that same or a similar feeling through the reins when we are on the horse, but for me, there's nothing quite like experiencing that same feeling from twenty feet away, connected only by two cotton lines.

Kathleen *Years and years ago, I was riding with Mark in a clinic, and he helped me with my hands. He took one end of the reins and I took the other, and he showed me how to provide my horse with a soft place to go. I'd never felt anything like that—on a horse or off. I didn't know one could do that with their hands and communicate so softly yet so very clearly with a horse. Feeling that softness and clarity come through the reins gave me something to shoot for in my own horsemanship, and I'm still working on it today.*

I've also had the opportunity to ride a couple of Mark's horses, and I get the same feeling from them that I got when Mark worked with my hands on the reins. There's always a soft place in there that Mark has helped the horse find, and when I ride them, all I have to do is find it and meet them there. I feel that, as a horseman, I am working on my hands every moment of the day, in everything I do. They'll never be as good as I want them to be, but they'll always be just a little better than before.

This picture is a really common sight when you're watching Mark ride. He's teaching someone in this photo, while also riding his horse. There's just enough tension in his hands to keep the reins from sliding through, and no more. There's information going from him to the horse and from the horse to him, and both are open to receiving that information. I guess that's the magic of that feel—that feeling of openness on our end and the openness on the horse's end.

Mark There's an old saying that states: "One cannot catch a bird with a closed hand." I have always liked this saying because it lends itself so well to horsemanship in so many ways. For instance, so much of what we do when we ride is based on developing a sense of softness between our horse and ourselves. When asked to describe what that sense of softness is, the analogy I most often use is that of holding a bird in your hand without crushing the bird, yet without letting the bird go.

Kathleen *This comes back to softness again. Softness isn't just a physical sensation, it's not just being relaxed in a structural way, though that's a small part of it. Softness comes down, in the end, to offering the best part of oneself to the horse. Many of us don't even know what the best parts of us are, and that makes it difficult for us to offer them. I think we also have to offer those best parts without any strings, without any expectation of getting something in return. It's a gift. And if we get that back from the horse—the best parts of him—we can accept it as a gift, just saying "thank you," rather than analyzing it and picking it apart.*

We can see that gift here—Mark and Tim are giving it to Tim's horse, Tico. Both men are soft, their hands open, the best parts of themselves on offer. Tico may not be able to return that gift just yet, but he will. That's not the point, anyway. The offer's been made.

Mark I am a firm believer that true softness doesn't come from the hands, it comes from the heart. By the same token, however, a horseman's hands are the conduit through which that softness can be transferred. For me, this photo is a perfect example of softness coming from the heart and being transferred to the horse through the hands. In this case, however, we're not just talking about one person and one set of hands, but two people and two sets of hands—at the same time. In this photo it is evident through our body language and position that both my friend Tim and I have this horse's best interest in mind, and we mean no harm. That feeling is being sent from our hands, through the ropes and to the horse. Each of our hands is offering the horse softness, perhaps all in a little different way, but softness nonetheless. The horse isn't able to accept that feel from us yet … but with consistency and time, he will.

Kathleen *As horsemen, most of us spend years and years trying to perfect the use of our hands, particularly in our riding. At Mark's clinics, we are often asked to help people with their hands, or with their horse's behavior in relation to the bridle. This photo was taken in Florida, and this is a horse and rider we had seen the previous year. The rider had asked the year before for help with stopping her horse softly, and that's what we'd worked on for four days. This horse had not had a lot of softness going on at the time, and neither had the rider. Here they are, a year later, and they're much softer. The rider's hands are open on the reins, something that was almost unthinkable a year ago. To me, this picture represents one of the great things about doing clinics—seeing the genuine progress people make while we're away working with others.*

Kathleen *This is equine chiropractor Dr. Dave Siemens again, and this is what he does for a living—he puts his hands on horses. There are lots of different types of people who practice lots of different kinds of healing arts with horses, and I think it's safe to say that most of them use their hands in some way. Dave is very generous with his expertise and he'll take the horse owner's hand and put it under his as he feels for movement in the horse. What's amazing is that Dave can still feel the joint and its movement through the owner's hand. I've learned a lot about feel from Dave and have been shown the degree of feel that's possible if we practice. Dave's hands are just like our hands, except he's practiced different things than most of us have.*

Mark I'm not sure how many times in the past twenty years I've seen Dr. Dave touch a horse in this manner. More times than not, after initially watching the horse move, he will slowly go around and gently place his hands on it, palpating the areas he sees as not having full range of motion. Within seconds he is able to diagnose and then treat the affected joint, often giving the horse immediate relief from pain or stiffness that the horse may have been struggling with for years. The sensitivity in Dave's hands is second to none, and every time I watch him work, I can't help but get the feeling I'm in the presence of a master who is meticulously practicing his craft.

Kathleen *This horse is Tico, a for-the-most-part-unhandled Mustang. One of the first things Mark wanted Tico to understand when they worked together was that Mark would not hurt Tico with his hands. It was very difficult for Tico to tolerate, much less enjoy, being touched by people. This photo was taken early on in the process that Mark was helping Tico with. We can see the wariness in Tico and the softness in Mark. Tico truly believed that people would hurt him someday. In order to function as a domestic horse, he was going to have to give up that belief, and that was a big deal to him. As Tico progressed in this work, Mark asked several of us who were watching to come and pet Tico at the end of each of his sessions, so he had people he didn't know well touching him. In the beginning of the process, Tico felt very tight under my hands when I petted him. His skin was tight and all the muscles underneath were tight. Within a few days, the feel of him got much softer, his skin loosened, and the muscles relaxed. But all that started with Mark's hands on the day this photo was taken.*

Mark It can be a pretty big deal for a worried horse to allow themself to be touched by a human. Yet, one of the first things we humans usually do when working with that same worried horse is try to get right up to him and then put our hands on him. One of the reasons for this, I suppose, is that the human animal uses its hands as a tool to help soothe and comfort other humans that are in some kind of distress. It's part of our nature. As such, we often assume a horse will just naturally feel better once we touch them. While that may be true in some cases, it isn't true in all cases, and it certainly wasn't true in Tico's case. A human hand approaching him was not very soothing to him at all, and in fact, was something to run away from.

In Tico's case, it was important to understand something about horses and the horse world that would ultimately help make a difference for him. There are two emotions that control horses from the day they're born to the day they die. These emotions are at opposite ends of a very broad spectrum. On one end of that spectrum is fear; on the other end is curiosity. A fearful horse can't be curious, and a curious horse can't be fearful. In Tico's case, we needed to turn his fear of the human hand into curiosity. Once he could become curious about it, it would then be easier for him to accept being touched by it.

In this photo I have extended my hand in a very soft manner, showing him there is no bad intent in it whatsoever. Still, I am not trying to touch him with it. When I first reached my hand out, Tico was nearly a foot away from it. I stood for several seconds with my hand outstretched in this way and eventually curiosity got the better of him. Here he has approached and, in smelling my hand, has gotten close enough with his muzzle to briefly touch my index finger a couple of times. At the point this photo was taken, I am ever so slightly reaching out with my index finger to reciprocate contact with him.

This was the very beginning of a process Tico would be going through, over the next few days in which he would not only learn to enjoy the touch of the human hand but soon he would even be searching it out.

Tools

ONE OF THE MOST IMPORTANT ASPECTS OF ANY JOB is the tools that we use. Working with horses is no different. Each person who works with horses has their own set of tools they are comfortable using. The tools I use are simple but effective and are made out of a variety of materials, from cotton to leather, metal, and even flesh and bone. Most of the tools I use have been with me for a very long time—in some cases, since I was a boy. Other tools are relatively new. Regardless, each one has been chosen for a very specific reason, and stays with me in the event it may be useful. Some of my tools I use almost every day, like my saddle, saddle pads, bridles, and ropes. Others, such as my spurs, have not been used in years. In fact, my spurs have hung on the wall in our family room for the past fifteen years—next to our branding iron that also doesn't get much use any more since we stopped hot-branding our horses and no longer run our own cattle.

Unless one of my training tools becomes broken beyond repair, I never throw anything out. By the same token, I also never go out and buy a tool just because it's the next new "thing." By keeping my tools at a minimum, to only the ones I feel are absolutely necessary for the type of work I do, I not only keep my tack rooms uncluttered, but also leave room to develop the most important tools I own … my own mind and body.

—M.R.

Kathleen When I got my first camera all those years ago, it came with a cheap but very fun Vivitar macro telephoto lens. I think that because I used that telephoto as my default lens during the formative stages of my photographic education, even today my eye naturally wants to break a scene down into various close-up pieces. I really like finding the little things that make a scene interesting to the eye.

Photographing the tools of our trade is a perfect place to do this, where shape, form, and texture are what give the tools life and interest in the photograph. Our tools tend to be worn in certain ways. For instance, Mark's cotton ropes have been to all the lower forty-eight states of the United States, plus The Netherlands, Belgium, Australia, England, and Scotland. They're soft and supple from use, and the fibers on the outside of the ropes are frayed from being dragged miles and miles in sand pens. Tooling in leather captures highlights and shadows. Dirt clings where dirt does. Straps carry black buckle marks where they get used a lot.

In this picture, we see quite a few tools, and they're in use. We have Mark's mohair reins, his lovely hand-made saddle, his felt saddle pad, his well-worn breast collar, his chaps with their handy knife pocket, and we can even see another tool of his trade—the wire that runs from his microphone headset to his transmitter that is hooked on his belt, out of view. Mark has chosen each of these tools for a reason, and each bear the marks of his unique usage.

Mark For years, my friend, saddlemaker Rusty May of Loveland, Colorado, has made my chaps for me. He knows that I use my equipment hard so he always uses good leather, and his stitches never fail. In this photo I'm wearing a new pair of Rusty's chaps that I received for Christmas. This was the first time I'd gotten a chance to wear them. The knife pouch on the left leg is something I have Rusty put on all my chaps for me. The knife inside is an Oldtimer, with an edge so sharp you could shave with it. We never know when we might have to cut through a rope, a piece of leather, string on a bale of hay, dig a splinter out of your hand, or even castrate a calf. In any of those cases, a good sharp knife is often the only tool that'll work. I'm right-handed, and it would be logical to put that pouch on the right side, however, because I am right-handed, I rope with my right hand, and if I'm dragging a calf to the fire, that pouch would get in the way.

My saddle was built by Gary Winckler of Deland, Illinois, and it's the most comfortable saddle I've ever sat in. On any given day, I'll be on my horse anywhere from three to ten hours. So a comfortable saddle is essential, not just for me, but also for my horse, which is why the saddle is built on a tree made by Dave Genadek. It is designed to fit the type of horses I ride most. Dave also built the breast collar.

Mark For many, many years I refrained from ever wearing sunglasses when I was working with, or around, horses. I wanted to make sure that the horses could see my eyes. But a few years back I began getting some pretty nasty headaches and my vision started to blur. Finally I broke down and went to the eye doctor, and he explained that the UV rays I had subjected myself to during all those years of standing in white, sandy arenas had begun to take their toll. He highly recommended I begin wearing a pair of good quality sunglasses anytime I was outside on a bright day. Reluctantly, I did what he recommended. Oddly enough, my headaches went away, as did the majority of my blurred vision. While some folks might look at wearing sunglasses as some sort of fashion statement, these days I actually have to look at them as just one more of the tools I need to perform my job properly. And the majority of the horses don't seem to mind, but if they do, I take them off.

Kathleen *The morning this photo was taken, we had a bit of a late start on the riding part of the day, so the light while Mark was tacking up was just fantastic. I sat on the tongue of a trailer nearby and just watched to see what would come up. When Mark took his saddle out of the trailer and swung it onto his hip, I started shooting, and this was the best of the bunch. This picture, to me, is one that epitomizes "the life," it symbolizes what we do—we saddle up and help other people with their horses. This picture is a bookend—this is how we start our day and this is how we end our day, most days of the year.*

Mark Here is a little different perspective on the saddle Gary made for me. I think this is one of the nicest photos Kathleen has ever taken, and it really shows the quality of Gary's work. It was the first time Gary had ever used the rope carving as a border on any of his saddles, and it is clearly visible here. By the time this photo was taken I had not had the saddle very long, yet it is already showing the signs of heavy use.

Kathleen *This picture was one of those opportunities to look at just a small part of a larger scene. It was early in the morning in Camp Verde, Arizona, in January, and Mark had tacked up his horse Rocky and tied him to a hitch-rail while we waited for the first clinic participant of the day. The light at that time of day was very stark and rather hard, but Mark's bridle was hanging mostly in shadow off of his saddle horn. The one part of the bridle that was highlighted by the sun was the tooling of the cheek piece. I started thinking about how, if we have any piece of equipment long enough, boy, could it tell some stories. So there are a bunch of stories here, in this little scene.*

Mark When I look at the tools in this photo, I think of my horse Buck, who was my partner for so many years. I have always liked the look of many of the old-style headstalls—wide cheek pieces and brow bands, leather conchos, and heavy buckles holding everything together. Many years ago I had my buddy Rusty May make this old-style headstall for Buck. Everybody who knows me knows I've never been a big one for a lot of fancy tooling on my tack…harder to keep clean, costs more, and doesn't do anything to improve the workability of the tool. However, for some reason, when I asked Rusty to make this particular headstall for Buck, I asked him to put this design on it. It is the only piece of tack I own with that much tooling. Looking back now, I believe I may have sub-consciously had it done to help bring attention to the head of that great, once-in-a-lifetime horse.

I stopped using this headstall for several years after Buck passed away and had only recently begun using it again on one of my new horses, Rocky. I bought Rocky from an old friend up in Minnesota, Lloyd Alm. Without knowing it until after I bought him, I found out Rocky's grand-mother on his dam's side was actually Buck's full sister.

Kathleen *When I first met Mark, I had been very involved in showing hunter and jumper show horses for about twenty years. Part of being a member of that culture for so long, I found, was the penchant I had for all sorts of gadgets and items of tack that were commonly used in "the business." One of the things that gradually happened as I spent time with Mark was that I ended up with two piles of gear—stuff I was likely to use at some point (a fairly small pile) and stuff I was unlikely to need any time soon (a pretty large pile). Now, I didn't throw that stuff out. There might be a horse down the line someday for which one of those gadgets might be just perfect. But I've come to see the value in using nice, simple gear that allows me to focus on communicating clearly with my horses. Heck, I sometimes have a hard enough time getting my message across that I don't need my tools modifying it. I still show my hunters at horse shows, but I carry a lot less gear now than I used to, and I kind of like it that way. I think the horses do, too.*

The cotton ropes that Mark uses, and which we see in this photo of Tim and Tico, were something I'd never seen before in the culture I came from, and when I first began using them, they felt foreign to me. But it didn't take long before I really liked the feel and life of the rope, and I would even pull mine out and ground-drive one of my horses just to practice handling the ropes.

Mark The tools I use have a tendency to be relatively simple and are usually made of things that are readily available to me. My "ground-driving/lunging rig," for instance, consists of nothing more than a nylon web halter with a sheepskin cover over the noseband, and two 32-foot cotton driving lines that I made myself. This rig has traveled all over the world with me and has been on thousands of horses over the years.

We horsemen often use our ropes without much thought. We handle lead ropes and reins and such every day, and just don't think about it a whole lot. This photo was taken at a clinic in California while Mark was explaining the use of the rope to the spectators. Again we see that Mark's hands are open, even though he's got some life in that rope. Mark's put a lot of time into learning to use his tools well, and ropes are no different. I'll often see him leading his horse and spinning the end of his lead rope, touching pebbles or leaves on the ground. Even then, he's practicing his craft.

Mark I am often asked about the tools I use, and the what and why of the choices I make regarding them. For instance, many folks these days use rope halters for their horses, while I have a tendency to use nylon web halters. Mostly, this is personal preference. I grew up using the flat halters, most of which back then were made of leather, and as a result, the flat halters are what I am comfortable using. Along those same lines, the flat web halters are a little more versatile for the type of work I usually need to do regarding halters, so they always seem to be my first choice.

The type of rope I choose to use most often, whether for my lead ropes or my driving/lunge lines, is made from good quality cotton. Again, this is the type of rope I grew up using, so I have a tendency to be a little more comfortable with it. However, I also like it because it's easy to work with, is less likely to burn either the handler or the horse should a stressful situation occur between the two, and is very easy to put life into and take life out of when necessary. In this photo one can easily see the life in the cotton rope and how little energy it takes to put that life in. It is also interesting to note the horse's relative indifference to the swinging of the rope. In this situation, the life in the rope is not directed toward the horse in any manner, whatsoever, so there's no need for her to feel worried or upset about its motion.

Mark   There are lots of "horse training" tools on the market these days, everything from huge balls used to desensitize a horse, to tiny clickers that you can hold between two of your fingers. While such tools absolutely have their place in the horse world, I feel sometimes they do distract from the training tools that are the most important of all—the human mind and body.

It's amazing the number of tools one *doesn't* need when the time is taken to hone our own mind and body. And it is also amazing to realize that many of the past experiences in our lives can easily dovetail into the work we do with horses, even though at first glance they may seem totally unrelated. In this photo, my friend Tim effortlessly and expertly tosses a rope over his horse's back. While Tim may not have had a tremendous amount of experience handling ropes around horses over the years, he has traveled over eighty thousand miles at sea. As a sailor, he spent many hours handling and using ropes, which now translates into his work with horses.

Kathleen *I've been studying the idea of softness ever since I met Mark more than a decade ago. The one thing I* do *know about softness is that the more I learn about it and work with it, the farther I see there is to go before I have a true understanding of it. Once I decided that softness was important to me as a horseman, I discovered it wasn't something I could just switch on when I was around horses, and switch off when I wasn't. It doesn't work that way. In order for me to be truly soft, I have to* live *soft, and that's really hard. As I go through the day, I try to see how softly I can do everyday things. Am I using just enough pressure to close the truck door? Am I gripping my water bottle harder than I need to in order to keep hold of it? Do things end up right where I intend to put them? Do I move efficiently and quietly? My degree of softness has a direct effect on the tools I come in contact with, be it the truck, my water bottle, or my horse training tools. My camera is yet another tool. If I'm soft, my mind is clear, and I can shoot almost without thinking. I can see something and let that idea in to take shape in my mind and shoot it in split seconds. The tighter or busier I am, the slower that idea is to take shape, and by the time I'm ready to act, the shot is gone.*

Tim is working again with cotton rope, sending messages to his horse Tico. He's clearly got an idea of what he's looking for, and he's putting those ideas through the rope to the horse. If we're soft, the tool can be more than a tool, it can be a conduit for thoughts and ideas, which is what I think we see here.

Mark I think the one thing that is most misunderstood about the use of tools is how the idea of "softness" translates from the human's hands, through the tool, to the horse, and then back. Well, for me, it starts with the *idea* of softness. Most of us are taught, and so we believe, that softness comes from the hands. It is my belief that softness is translated through the hands, but it doesn't start there. Softness comes from the heart. For me, this is a great picture of softness coming from the heart, and being translated through the hand, through the tool, and ultimately to the horse. On the other end of the tool, and even though we can't see the horse, we know he is sending softness back by the way the rope is reacting. If one looks closely, we can actually see there is an ever so slight amount of slack in the rope while Tim asks Tico to turn while being ground-driven. This slack, even though very small, lets us know the signal from Tim to Tico has been received, understood, and is now being responded to in a soft manner.

Kathleen *I learned to know this bag and its contents very well in the two and a half years I worked full-time for Mark. Every morning when we were working, I'd get the bag out and put it by the round pen or the arena we'd be in for the day, so seeing that bag sitting by the fence means "ready to go to work" to me.*

Mark For years I have carried all my "groundwork" tools in a bag just like this. The vast majority of the tools in the bag have been with me for years; in the case of some of my ropes, nearly twenty years. They are well worn, as one can plainly see here. The bag itself, however, looks new, because it is. Generally speaking, the bag I carry the tools in gets replaced about every three or four years due to general wear and tear.

Kathleen *One of the things I like about a telephoto lens is that I don't have to physically insert myself into a scene to shoot it. I'm often able to shoot close-ups like this from the sidelines, where I won't intrude into what's going on. I've also done quite a bit of shooting from horseback, with my camera bag slung over the horn. I like the idea of taking pictures of horses from horseback, it's just fitting. This is a little different view of some of the same tools we've seen before, in particular, Mark's saddle and bridle. I was looking at the shape of the stirrup from this angle and the little brass nails along the footbed. Changing the angle that we view an object from can change what we notice about it and how we see it. I guess the same is true of horses, and of life in general.*

Kathleen *It seems like chaps and saddles are the quintessential symbols of horsemen's tools, so I wanted to have a photo in the collection that showed the wear on Mark's chaps. We use our chaps for riding, for putting up hay, and to protect our jeans from the everyday dirt and wear and tear of being around horses. So they get quite a bit of hard use. Each of us wear our tools a certain way—the wear on Mark's chaps is different from mine, and the wear on my boots is different from his. It's the wear and the dirt and the scars that tell the story in the end.*

Mark I'm not sure how many miles I have ridden in these chaps. Rusty made them for me back in 2001 and they, like my ropes and some of my other tools, have been all over the world. While the chaps are well worn, the boots I'm wearing are relatively new. They seemed very comfortable when I first tried them on, but by the time this photo was taken … I wasn't too sure.

Splashed White

AT A CLINIC IN GEORGIA, we were presented with a horse that appeared to have "spooking" issues. The owner told us he could be very unpredictable out on the trails and had a tendency to run off once something frightened him. He also had a tendency to panic when she turned him out into the pasture, particularly if she turned him out at night.

We worked with the gelding on the first day and found him to be everything that the owner said he was—spooky and pretty over-reactive to most stimuli. At first glance, I felt as though the horse had mentally "shut down." The type of mental shut down I thought we were seeing usually shows up in horses that have gone through a severely traumatic or abusive period in its life (which, according to the owner, this horse had). Often the trauma or abuse could be so severe that a horse's only coping mechanism was to shut down mentally, and sometimes physically, just to survive. Unfortunately, even when the horse is moved on to a better situation, the mental shut down in the horse remains. The horse often will remain shut down when being ridden or handled. That is, of course, right up until something "wakes him up," at which time he often spooks or panics uncontrollably for no apparent reason. This particular horse showed all the classic signs of a mentally shut down horse. However, one night after supper, Kathleen and I sat down and compared notes on the horse, and ultimately came up with a completely different idea for where the unpredictable behavior was coming from.

—M.R.

Mark One of the things that troubled me about this horse right from the start, besides his somewhat unpredictable behavior, was the way he held his ears. Not only did they appear to be placed slightly in front and just below where a horse's ears should be placed, but he didn't seem to move them around much either—like most horses do when searching for the source of a certain sound.

When Kathleen and I sat down after dinner on the second day of the clinic to chat, she mentioned almost in passing that she thought this paint horse might actually be a Splashed White paint. For those who don't know, Kathleen is somewhat of an expert when it comes to horse colors, a skill she picked up and honed over the years, and which she uses extensively in her work as an artist. Me, I'm pretty good at the blacks, browns, reds, and yellows. But beyond that, I get a little lost. So the term "Splashed White" paint admittedly didn't mean much to me, or even ring a bell for that matter.

I guess I looked at her long enough with a blank expression on my face, because before long she went on to explain that one of the inherent traits of the Splashed White paint horses is that … they are born deaf. Suddenly, this horse's unpredictable behavior and the strange placement of his ears began to make perfect sense.

The very next day when the paint horse came into the arena, I stood next to him, near his shoulder, and reached up and snapped my fingers just behind his ears. There was absolutely no response from him. I repeated this a number of times with exactly the same non-reaction from him. Then I went over to my horse, Rocky, who was standing nearby, and did the same thing. Rocky's ears flicked back in sync with the snapping of my fingers. It wasn't all that scientific of an experiment, but it certainly showed us what we needed to know.

Kathleen *This situation with the Splashed White horse was important for me because in this case I just happened to, accidentally, have a piece of seemingly unrelated information—almost trivia—that was key to understanding this horse. I suppose that I never really considered that my knowledge of equine color genetics could actually help a horse in a training context someday. But horsemanship is life—there is no line between them. We never know what piece of information will be important, and if we come across it and it sticks—I bet there will be a reason for that someday.*

In this horse's case, he'd had some odd struggles in his life. If people or things appeared behind him suddenly, he would kick out. If he was turned out in his pasture after dark, he could not find the other horses and would frantically pace the fence line. His owner would have to take a flashlight out there and help him find them. She didn't know why he had trouble with these things, but once she understood that he was deaf, all those odd problems started to make sense. Now, he's not a "problem horse," he doesn't have "issues," he's just deaf, and that's not his fault.

Mark This photo clearly shows the inherent traits of the Splashed White. White appears horizontally across the bottom half of the body and tail, while the top of the horse is primarily dark. He has a bald, white head and two blue eyes. It also shows the peculiar position of the horse's ears.

The Job

I HAVE OFTEN THOUGHT OF HOW LUCKY I AM to be able to do the kind of work that I do. Not only do I get to make my living working with horses, but I also get to travel, meet new people, and see a lot of the world I probably wouldn't get to see if I was doing something else. Giving horsemanship clinics is a pretty special job, and right now I wouldn't trade it for any other. However, on the other hand, I came to realize a long time ago that, in the end (and in many ways), clinicing *is* just a job, just like any other job.

I have had a number of folks throughout the years tell me how they would switch jobs with me in a heartbeat if they could. I suppose that's because in its own way, clinicing can look and sound somewhat glamorous, particularly to the casual observer. But usually those folks that want to switch jobs have only gotten to see the "finished product," as it were … the time we spend working with the horses and riders while at the venue in their area. What they don't see is the somewhat less glamorous side of clinicing: the long hours driving or flying from one venue to another, the early mornings and late nights, the planning of the logistics of traveling with horses, particularly in times of bad weather, as well as working out the details of scheduling and routing. Most of all, what they don't get a chance to see is all the countless hours away from family, friends, and home.

What follows is a brief chronicle of what clinicing is for us, a sort of behind the scenes look at a job that I believe is like no other, yet at the same time, is like any other.

—M.R.

Kathleen *Being in the truck on the road for days at a stretch can, understandably, be a bit tedious. The trip from home in Colorado to Florida is almost three days; most locations on the West Coast are about twenty-one hours drive time from home. That's a lot of time spent in a truck, just driving. Mark and I have passed many hours on the road visiting about this and that, listening to CDs or the radio, and in companionable silence.*

Traveling great distances with horses is a logistical three-ring circus. Each state in the United States has slightly different rules about the Coggins Test and health certificate requirements for visiting horses. Colorado and some other western states also require brand certificates. Within the week preceding our departure, each clinic horse's paperwork is checked, updated, and organized. Vet and brand inspector visits are scheduled. National weather patterns are checked, and routes proposed. All that planning can go out the window if there are unexpected weather or traffic problems. But in my time with Mark, we've never been late to where we've needed to go, the paperwork's always been in order, and the horses have always traveled well. By the time we get to a venue, we're usually ready to settle down for just a bit, and I think the horses are, too.

Mark The easy part of our job happens after we have arrived at the venue and we get an opportunity to meet and work with the riders and their horses. The part that can sometimes be a little challenging is actually *getting* to the venue, particularly in the winter months, due to the unpredictability of the weather. Living in Colorado presents some interesting logistics regarding the ability to get in or out of the state during the winter. Much of my travel in the winter takes me to the Southeast or Southwest of the United States, which means I may either need to travel through the eastern plains of Colorado or over the high mountain passes. Either way, the chances of getting caught in a spring snow storm are usually very good, as we can see in this photo.

We are traveling through Glenwood Canyon, about one hundred and fifty miles west of Denver. We had just passed through blizzard and whiteout conditions traveling over Vail Pass on I-70 on our way to southern California in March. By the time we got into this canyon, the storm had calmed down considerably, but the road was still a little icy and snowpacked, which can make traveling with a sixty-foot rig a little dicey if you're not careful.

When Kathleen took this photo, we were still more than one thousand miles away from our destination, about seven hundred miles from where we planned on stopping for the night, and due to the storm we had just passed through, we were two hours behind schedule. Still, the road stretches out in front of us, and with luck, we'll make up the lost time between now and when we get to where we're going.

Mark This photo was taken less than fifteen hours from when the previous photo was taken. Here we are traveling on I-15 through the Mohave Desert, just south of Baker, California. There was a seventy-degree difference in temperature between when we left Colorado the day before, and when Kathleen snapped this picture. The kind of heat we experienced in the Mohave that day would be indicative of the temperatures we and our horses would be dealing with during the entire trip. Our horses were still haired up from the Colorado winter, but by the time we headed home they had pretty much shed out … just in time to deal with the cool temperatures of spring in the Rockies.

Mark Often when we do clinics, we run into participants who are near panic stricken at the prospect of riding their horses in front of a bunch of spectators who have come to watch what's going on. Having noticed this early on in my career, I took to the habit of opening gates for the riders as they entered the arena whenever the opportunity arose. I try to do this as a small gesture of welcome, and it sometimes gives me the opportunity to say something as a sort of icebreaker before we get down to the business of working with them and their horses. I'm not sure how much effect it has on calming anybody down, if any … but it sure never hurts, either.

Kathleen *Clinic horses learn quickly to conserve their energy for their work. Their days can easily stretch to ten hours, maybe in heat or in cold, with much of that time spent under the saddle. They might do that day after day, with their "days off" spent in the trailer commuting to the next clinic, for three weeks at a stretch. This photo was taken early in the morning on a rare day off in Arroyo Grande, California. It seems uncanny to me that from the moment Mark's horses arrived at this venue, they had not run in that field. But on the morning of their day off, that's the first thing they did—have a good, feet-in-the-air, snorting, tail-flipping, side-heaving run. How did they know it was their day off?*

Kathleen *I have a whole new appreciation for working horses since I began to use my horse to help me in my job rather than to entertain myself as a hobby. This sight is very common at Mark's clinics—clinic horses quietly standing tied somewhere. I never used to think horses could do this, just stand tied for long periods of time, without getting in some sort of trouble. I came to clinicing from an equestrian culture where we just didn't do things like that. These horses don't paw, they don't bang on the trailer, and they don't chew on each other's tack. They just stand and wait patiently. This IS their work, to wait. I believe that they come to understand what their job description is, and it may be fanciful, but I think they may actually appreciate simply having a job to show up for. I think I've even seen horses take pride in their clinic horse job. Even this job—standing tied—done well is a big deal, really.*

Mark A big part of our clinic horses' job is learning how to be patient. They spend hours on end inside the trailer and can spend even more hours tied to the outside of it. Often we will stop late at night in some busy truck stop or rest area somewhere, jump them out of the trailer and tie them up so they can eat out of a hay bag, while we catch some much-needed sleep in the trailer living quarters. In the morning, they will go back in the trailer and stand for several more hours before we get to where we're going.

During the clinic, they will stand tied to the trailer in the morning while we're tacking them up, and they will stand there again during our lunch break. Sometimes they will stand tied to a fence post or simply be left alone in the middle of an arena, expected to stand and wait, while we help a rider with some issue they have with their horse on the ground or in the round pen.

While this photo may simply look like two horses standing tied to a trailer, what it really is a picture of is two working horses performing a very important part of their job … being patient.

Kathleen *Being on the road is a very unique way of life. When I first started traveling with Mark, I didn't know if I would like it or not. I thought that the constant change might make me feel unsettled or rudderless. But what I found is that the consistency we crave in our lives can come from within us; it does not have to come from what is around us. In this job, we may spend four days in one place, travel one day, and then spend four days in another place. During those four days there's a whole lot of people, riders and spectators alike, whose names we learn and stories we hear. We become a part of their lives and they a part of ours for four days. Then we leave and do it again elsewhere. We're constantly getting to know people, and just as we get to know them a little bit, it's time for us to move on.*

Mark always makes time for people, answering questions, hearing stories about their horses, and signing books. Those things are important to them. Many people have a story about how Mark's books have helped them with their horses or in their life, and they want him to know that. This photo was taken in California as Mark took some time out to sign a few books for these women during lunch hour.

Mark I have never really considered myself an author. Even when I was writing my first book all those years ago, I looked at it simply as writing a book, nothing more, nothing less. I really had no idea what writing that book might hold for the future, and in some ways, I didn't give much thought to the fact that people might actually want to buy it, read it, and perhaps even want me to sign it. Actually, I was so surprised the first time someone asked me to sign a book that my hand shook a little as I scribbled down the inscription. That was a long time ago, and I've gotten more settled about performing that part of my job since then. I still wouldn't necessarily say I've gotten used to the idea, but I'm definitely not near as nervous about it these days as I once was.

Kathleen *In January, we did some work for a place outside of Las Vegas that provided trail rides to the public. The clinic there was a private one, in that the dude-string owner had brought Mark in to help his employees (wranglers) learn how to work with the horses better. There were no spectators, and Mark didn't wear a microphone. The dude string was still working while we were there, so the wranglers would come and go, sometimes working with us and sometimes taking clients out for rides. We worked on everything from catching, to adjusting equipment, to riding issues. It was a unique working environment, and it very much felt like we were a bunch of friends just getting together to mess with horses.*

Every morning, the horses that were going to work that day had to be brought from the pasture, up the canyon to the hitch-rail area, where they would wait for riders to come. It was probably a quarter of a mile from the pasture to the hitch rails, and it was open country, so the horses had to be led up. Rather than making multiple trips, the wranglers took a string of half-a-dozen horses and tied one horse to the next by tying its lead rope around its neighbor's neck. This made a "chain" of horses that one wrangler could then pony up the canyon. I'd never seen anything like that in all my time in horses, six or seven horses abreast, tied together and calmly walking on by. When I saw that, I knew I had to shoot it because I'd probably never see anything like it again.

Mark There was a time, not so long ago, when if someone needed to move a string of horses from one place to another, they would simply tie them all together and pony the whole bunch using the horse they were riding. It was a pretty common practice among horse traders in the 1800s and even into the early to mid-1900s. It's not such a common practice these days, however, and can be an unusual sight when you come across someone who is still doing it. This was just part of the morning routine at the dude ranch. These horses were expected to do this part of their job without worry and without hesitation—be tied together and walk quietly from one place to another as a group—and they did. No big deal, no fancy training, just a job that needed to be done properly in order for the day to progress.

Kathleen *The most obvious and visible part of Mark's job is the teaching part. Although I guess you could call him a "horse trainer," what he really does is work mostly with people so they can do whatever it is they want to do with their horses a little better. Being a good teacher, I think, starts with compassion. A student is in a vulnerable position because they're asking for help and trusting that they'll be taken care of, both mentally and physically, while they get that help. That's a lot of responsibility for a teacher. It's a responsibility I know Mark takes seriously. Our job starts with first doing no harm. That might sound trite, but we have to start there. We first do no harm, and then maybe we can help from there.*

In this photo, Mark is helping a rider with her hands so she can get a feel for softness. She'll take the feel Mark is showing her back to her horse in a moment. While Mark is doing this, he's also fully aware of the activity going on in the background, and if he were to need to handle something back there, he could do so. We've had discussions about this, and it comes down to being aware and using all of one's senses. Mark may not be able to see what's going on behind him, but he can hear everything clearly and can tell where everything is and what is happening by the sounds he hears.

Mark It's hard to say how much time during a clinic we actually spend on our own horses, and how much time we spend afoot helping someone from the ground. I suppose if I had to guess, on some days it might be as much as fifty-fifty. Regardless, there are just some times when no matter how much we try to explain a thought or concept to someone, the only way for it to really be understood is for us to get down and show them. One of those sometimes-difficult-to-grasp concepts is the idea of using pressure through the reins, without pulling on the horse. For me, this is at the very heart of developing softness between a horse and rider, and is one of those things that, unless the rider actually feels what we are talking about, they may not be able to understand it. Usually, all it takes is a few minutes of feeling "pressure without pull" for the rider to get a better idea of what we are asking him or her to do, and from there, progress in softness is often made in leaps and bounds.

Kathleen *Mark really strives for the students to do as much of the work by themselves as possible. After all, when the clinic is over, we leave. The student will still have the horse and needs to be able to work with it. But there are times when it is helpful to physically show a student how to do something, and there are times when the student is perhaps not in a place where they can do the work that the horse requires at that moment. Mark does not ride students' horses for them; he stopped doing that years ago. He found that when he was riding people's horses for them, they came back year after year with the same problems. When he stopped riding their horses, and instead taught* them *how to work through the issues, the next time he saw them, those issues were gone.*

Mark says he's still working on how to teach people ground work in a way where he doesn't have to step in. I'm sure he'll get that done someday, but until then, I always enjoy watching him work. Here he helps his friend Tim with his Mustang, Tico. Mark always had Tim finish the work with Tico, but Mark was there to step in if he was needed. Teaching is a balancing act in a lot of ways. We need to be able to step in when needed, and only when needed. Too little help isn't help at all. Too much help isn't help either. Mark has told me many times, "It's all about offering the right information at the right time." Simple idea, but not easy to do.

Mark This is another one of those times when being on the ground was not only helpful, but necessary. My friend Tim and I are working with Tico, helping him to accept ropes around and over his body. Tico was a pretty nervous horse, and while Tim had already done quite a bit of work with Tico and ropes, the gelding still had some wariness about the whole idea. At this point, I'm explaining the timing of how we want the rope to move as it makes contact with Tico's body. The way a rope moves on or around a horse may sound trivial to us, but for a nervous horse it can be the difference between understanding and panic. Shortly after this photo was taken, Tim stepped back in and was able to help Tico through the rough spot he was having trouble with. Just by the little adjustment he made from this conversation, Tim was able to talk Tico down from a very worrisome place, and to progress nicely with his training.

Mark I enjoy working with riders of all different skill levels, from raw beginners to the upper-level dressage or upper-level western rider. In this photo, I'm working with one of those students that falls in the middle. She had been riding for a while, had a very nice horse that she had done a lot of good work with, and was completely comfortable riding her … as long as she was in the round pen and the two of them were traveling at a walk. Riding outside the round pen made her a little nervous. But rather than worrying about what she *couldn't* do with her horse (ride outside the round pen), she cheerfully worked on the things she *could* do while inside the pen. She spent time developing a good walk, stop, back, and turn, as well as teaching her horse to follow her properly while being led. Many of the folks we work with—often some of the most experienced—get so focused on what they *can't* do with their horses that they have trouble seeing what they *can* do.

I suppose it's just an illusion of perspective. The more experience some folks have, the more pressure they put on themselves and their horses to perform at a high level, and the less fun they seem to have. On the other hand, here was this relatively inexperienced gal, riding at a walk in the round pen, not worried about this, that, or the other, and just happy to be spending time with her horse on a sunny afternoon. To me, that's what working with horses is all about.

Mark There is a look a rider gets on their face when it's clear they grasp the information that is being presented. Their eyes light up, the face softens, and a little smile begins to spread. In this photo, I was discussing the idea of footfall and cadence with one of the participants in a weeklong clinic in California. At first I wasn't sure if what I was saying was being understood. Then suddenly her expression began to change, and at that moment Kathleen got this photo from clear across the arena. A big part of our job is taking the time to see that riders leave with the information they came for. We always know we've done our part when this kind of expression crosses the rider's face.

Quiet

HORSEMANSHIP CLINIC VENUES, just by their nature, are relatively hectic places. There are horse trailers coming and going, people carrying chairs here and there, cell phones ringing, conversations going on, dogs barking, and any number of other major or minor distractions. Even so, all of the activity is punctuated by brief and sometimes sustained moments of quiet. These moments show up in a variety of ways.

There is a certain kind of quiet at a clinic venue in the morning before everyone comes to work for the day. There's another kind of quiet at the end of the day when everyone leaves. There's the quiet that happens when we teach by touching rather than by using words. There's the quiet that happens between a horse and a rider when their minds become still and uncluttered by the who, what, when, where, and why.

The photos that follow are examples of the quiet that can happen at a clinic venue, even when things that are going on all around are not.

—M.R.

80

Friends

BACK IN 1993, my first book *Considering the Horse: Tales of Problems Solved and Lessons Learned,* was released. Until then, I was just this guy up in the mountains of Colorado that messed with horses, and no one, myself included, had any idea if anything would ever come of that little book. Within just a few years of that book's release, however, my quiet little life up in the hills took a pretty dramatic change.

Since that time way back when, I have gone from working one little ranch to another, to a life on the road, traveling all over the world helping folks with their horses. Over the years, my job has taken me to just about every state in the United States, as well as several countries in Europe, Great Britain, and Australia. For the most part, my job is a great one to have, and while the travel and being away from home and family is always difficult, the friends I have met along the way have somehow made it all worth it.

In the photos that follow are some examples of a few of those friends I have met over the years. Whether those relationships have been with other people, people and their horses, or horses with other horses, one thing has always been constant … wherever I go in the world, I always know I am bound to walk away having met someone I can call a friend.

—M.R.

Kathleen *This is Jo and her horse Quinn, and I took this and the following photos in England in July. Jo and her mother had ridden a couple of times with Mark in England previously, so they and their horses were familiar faces to us at this point. Jo and Quinn share a bond that's unique to young girls and their horses; I think it's a special kind of friendship we can only have with horses when we're teenage girls. These two create a lovely picture of intimacy and contentment, and I bet she'll remember her friendship with Quinn for the rest of her life.*

Kathleen When I first began traveling with Mark, I had never traveled long distances with horses before, or used my horse as an essential part of my work. Traveling with your horse day in and day out creates a unique bond between the two of you. After all, in the life of a clinic horse, the only bit of consistency in that life is his handler. The environment, schedule, food, and weather may all be different, but we need to remain constant for them, to the best of our ability.

I remember going down the road with Mark not long after I'd begun traveling with him. We were chatting about this and that, and at one point, he told me that although his clinic horse, Mouse, was back in the trailer, he still felt like they were connected, even right then. I've often thought about that. It's one of the marks of a good friendship, isn't it—that feeling of being connected even when you're not together.

On the following pages is a series of photos of Mark and his clinic horse, Rocky, that I took not long after they began working together, and I love the little story it tells. This whole interaction took maybe ten seconds; it's just a tiny glimpse into a typical ten-hour day. But it tells a lot about the promising friendship developing between these two.

These moments are what I tried to keep an eye out for while I was shooting. In these very commonplace actions, between obvious events, are truth and hope and certainty.

Mark Kathleen took these photos in Florida in January. My new horse, Rocky, and I had just started working together a few weeks before and were still in the process of feeling each other out by the time we got to this venue. Even with that, I had already found that I really liked this horse. He was honest, willing, and he tried very hard to do whatever was being asked of him, even though his new job with me was completely foreign to him.

I noticed when getting Rocky out of his pasture on this particular morning that he had a slight swelling under his right eye—probably from a fire-ant bite, and those ants can be a little nasty down in that part of the country. He didn't really complain about it much throughout the day, but it was clear the eye was uncomfortable to him. In this series, I had dismounted to demonstrate something to a student, and the student had since ridden off to try what we had just talked about.

In the first photo, I am watching the student go, and as I turned my head I caught a glimpse of the swelling in Rocky's eye and noticed it seemed to be a little worse than it had been that morning.

In the second photo, for just this split second, my full attention has gone to his eye to see if what I caught in my initial glimpse is actually what is going on. In the third photo, my attention is back on the rider, while asking Rocky to bring his head toward me so I can get a closer look. At this point it is clear the rider is doing okay with the task I asked her to perform, so once again my attention has gone back to Rocky's eye.

In the fourth photo a fly has also started paying attention to Rocky's eye, and I have reached up to brush it away. While my hand is there, I also wipe the eye clean of some dried discharge that had started to develop. A few seconds later, in the fifth and final photo, the rider is now once again in need of my attention, so it is time for both Rocky and I to go back to work.

As I said earlier, I really like this horse, and I know how hard life on the road can be for him, or any horse I travel with. Because of that, I like to try to make their time with me as comfortable as possible—whenever possible—even if it means doing something as simple as wiping the dirt away from a sore eye. This gesture may not seem like much, and maybe it isn't. But as far as I'm concerned, there is certainly nothing wrong with taking a little time out of the day to give a hand to a new friend.

Kathleen *This is Tim and Trudy, and I took this photo of them together while they were watching Mark and a student work at a clinic in Florida. I have a hard time taking photos of people I don't know because I feel (rightly or not) like I'm intruding on them. I've found that once I get to know someone, I feel more comfortable taking their picture. Tim, Mark, Trudy, and I became good friends during our eleven days together. We spent our days working horses together and our evenings sharing meals. I got to know them well enough that I felt comfortable shooting this moment between them, where we can see their singular friendship.*

Mark This is a great picture of friends Tim and Trudy. It's a peaceful scene, which for me shows the caring that somehow seems only available to those couples who start as good friends, then eventually have that friendship grow into something very special between them. Whether with a horse or another human, we should all be so lucky.

Kathleen *Another part of a clinic horse's job is to get along with whomever his equine friend happens to be on that trip. I've traveled with a horse who didn't necessarily get along well with others, and that made a tough job even harder for everyone, especially for the other horses along on the trip. It's very important to do everything efficiently on the road because wasted energy is missed at the end of a trip. The two horses in this photograph are traveling together for the first time on the trip this photo was taken, and they didn't really know each other previously. I carried my camera everywhere I went while working with Mark, and when I came out first thing one morning, there these guys were, clearly friends, sleeping pretty soundly in the sun before the start of the day. A clinic horse learns quickly to drink when offered water, eat when offered food, and sleep every chance he gets. He'll be back at work before he knows it.*

Mark We took a trip to California in March to do a series of clinics starting in Arroyo Grande, and ending in the L.A. area. Over the past two years when Kathleen and I traveled together, she would always bring one of her horses, and I brought one, or sometimes two, of mine. During that time, the horses we traveled with had always known each other pretty well, having lived with one another for years. However, in the late fall and early winter of the previous year, all that changed. About that time I had purchased some new horses and planned on using them for a number of jobs, from being on the road with me, to helping out with our week-long clinics, to general ranch and trail work.

Most of these horses went out on winter pasture together and got an opportunity to get to know one another there. However, because I was going to be using Rocky (my new clinic horse) right away, he stayed on the home place and didn't get to know any of the other horses. On this trip to California, I brought Rocky and Doc, one of the horses that had previously been on winter pasture. Before this trip, Rocky and Doc did not get much of a chance to get to know one another … we just jumped them both in the trailer and took off. At first, when turned out together there were the usual snorts and squeals one would expect from two new horses. But within just a couple days of traveling together, Rocky and Doc soon became good buddies. Kathleen took this photo one morning before we started work, and the friendship already developing between them is pretty evident.

103

Kathleen *This is Tim and his Mustang, Tico, and they share a pretty extraordinary friendship. When I first met Tim, I wondered at his dedication to this troubled horse, but once I met Tico, I understood quite a bit better. Tim and Tico have what many of us long for in our horse/human relationships: Tim is head-over-heels in love with this horse, and this horse is starting to believe Tim has the answers to his questions. What's pretty astonishing about this photo is the expression on these two friends' faces—they match exactly. Those of us who love horses believe this kind of connection is possible between us, and it's that belief that fuels our passion. We strive and work and practice to get that connection. But all this man did, I think, to get that connection was to open his heart to this horse.*

Mark Tim and Tico have a pretty special bond between them. It's the kind of bond nearly everyone we come in contact with seems to be searching for. At the time this photo was taken, Tico was not exactly sure of what his place was in the world of humans. Even with that, he seemed to somehow understand that this particular human wasn't so bad. Tim has given the best of himself to this horse since he first took ownership of him, and he continues to do so every day. This is a very difficult thing for many humans to do because many folks don't even know what the best of themselves is. Yet, Tim seems to be a natural at it. He undoubtedly has this horse's best interest in mind, and it shows. He doesn't push his idea of a relationship on this horse, but rather he gently guides him into a different way of thinking and feeling. It is that commitment to *allowing* a connection to develop with his horse that is turning the relationship from one of worry and self doubt, to one of confidence and trust. I agree with Kathleen. In this photo, and in the one that follows, it appears both Tim and his horse have the same expression on their face … and that's just not something you get to see every day.

Kathleen *This photo of Tim and Tico was taken only seconds after the previous photo. I think their expressions match exactly once again. Tim and Tico were easy to shoot because there was so much emotion in everything they did together. Tim wears his heart on his sleeve, and Tico just doesn't know how to be anything but brutally honest. That emotion has been diluted through reproduction in a photograph, so if there is still emotion left in this photo, it was present exponentially in the actual moment.*

People were attracted to this pair during this Florida clinic. "When are Tim and Tico working?" I'd hear people say during the day. During Tim and Tico's sessions, the round pen was ringed with interested faces, and people jumped at the chance to pet this great horse and talk to Tim about the horse's breeding and heritage. It's interesting that people were attracted to them so inextricably, and I wonder if it wasn't their longing for the openness that these two share that drew them.

While we're on the road, we don't usually get many days off because Mark likes to schedule clinics and travel time as efficiently as possible. This photo was taken on a rare day off when these three guys, Mark, Tim Harvey (center), and Jim Wooldridge (right), got together to work with their horses in the afternoon. One way or another, nearly every moment on the road revolves around horses. Here these guys are, when they could be doing something else, working horses. I liked this casual picture of three guys sharing an afternoon together, brought together far from home by horses.

Mark For us, the term "day off" is actually a pretty relative term. I say this because even though we may not actually be clinicing on those particular days, it doesn't necessarily mean we aren't working. Often on our "day off" we might be traveling from one venue to another, which could be up to eight hundred miles away from the last. We might be doing a demo of some kind, or cleaning equipment, or looking at someone's troubled horse, or doing laundry, or performing any number of other essential tasks one needs to take care of while living on the road.

On this particular day, my buddies—Tim Harvey and "Big" Jim Wooldridge—and I decided to spend some time working with a couple of horses. There are times when I really miss getting a chance to work like this—no microphone, no auditors, no schedule—just some friends and some horses on a warm, sunny afternoon in Florida. As I recall, we whiled away the better part of that afternoon hanging out at the round pen, telling some jokes that weren't all that funny—and some that were—and getting some good work done with some pretty nice horses.

Kathleen *Every once in a while when we're doing our work out on the road, we meet a horse and rider combination who share a very special friendship. This pair, from Devon, England, made quite an impression on me. The horse was a huge blue roan draft horse, and for a living, he worked in a logging operation. The woman in the picture had borrowed him to ride in the clinic with Mark, and she was so tiny that her legs barely reached down his massive barrel. It looked like she was straddling a picnic table. But that horse would do anything for her, and she for him. They may have made a very physically incongruous picture together, but it was all at once harmonious as well. He was just happy to be around her, and she was happy to be out in the countryside riding. I was lucky to catch this little exchange between them as she finished her session and handed him back to his owner.*

Kathleen *I met Carl Hill for the first time in early 2005, and that hysterical first meeting certainly has set the tone for the remainder of our friendship. Carl's the kind of guy who will answer the phone, having no idea who's on the other end, and say, "Hey, whatcha wearing?" But he's also a closet philosopher, and while I was going through a divorce in 2005, he told me that he loves his job taking care of the ranch he lives on with his wife, Anita Parra. "It just makes me happy to see Anita happy, it's that simple," he told me. He may not have thought he was giving me advice at the time, but he was.*

Mark Every year since 2001, I have made an annual trip to Arroyo Grande, California, to do some clinics for my friends Anita Parra, and her husband Carl Hill. Carl and I have become pretty good pals over the years. He is a fun guy to be around, mostly due to his great sense of humor, and we always seem to do a lot of laughing when we are around each other. However, as funny as Carl is, he also has a pretty thoughtful side to him as well, and it comes out almost by accident from time to time. In my book *Horsemanship Through Life,* I took the opportunity to use some of his thoughtful insight as the main theme in the last chapter, which was titled "Price of the Ticket." Going to Carl and Anita's place is always one of the highlights of my year. The clinics are always good, the riders and horses are always great, and Carl and I get to spin some yarns, tell some lies, and generally have ourselves a pretty good time—even though we both know we may be having too much fun whenever Miss Anita rolls her eyes, shakes her head, and starts speaking Spanish in our general direction.

Mark

I T WAS INEVITABLE THAT DURING THE COURSE OF THIS PROJECT, I ended up with quite a few photos of Mark himself. All of the photos in this book tell the story of who Mark is because any photo of Mark working is a photo of who he is.

In these photos, the viewer will see Mark as I see him, by necessity, since they reflect my own point of view through the lens. Someone else may, rightly so, see him differently, and that's okay. These pictures are Mark as I know him.

—K.L.

Kathleen *This photo is from a series I shot in California in March. Mark doesn't get many quiet moments like this while he's working because he operates on the assumption that "if you can see me, I'm available." People will often stop by while he's doing other things to ask questions, or have him sign a book, or tell him a story that's important to them. Simple tasks like tacking up can be interrupted several times. It's interesting to watch, because Mark gets everything done that he needs to get finished, on time, and never steps on anyone in the process. I think that's because he can blend with what comes to him while at the same time moving in the direction he needs to go. Everything around Mark has a flow to it, it's deliberate and conscious and purposeful, and I hope that these photos reflect that.*

Kathleen *Mark likes to do as much of his work himself as he can. As his assistant, I expected him to leave me with lots of jobs he didn't have time for, but in reality, I found myself having to beat him to jobs to save him from doing them. He especially likes to catch, groom, saddle, and then put away his own horse. He drives his own truck as much as he can, sets up his own P.A. as much as he can, and generally just doesn't expect others to do for him what he can do himself. I have learned a lot about hard work during my time with Mark, and also the idea of working hard because one wants to, not because one has to. There are all kinds of things during the day that we could just not do, and no one would notice. Regardless, I think Mark would do those things anyway.*

Kathleen *Mark likes kids a lot, and a couple of years ago, Mark did a "penny trick" for these two girls in California. In the trick, Mark has the girls stand next to each other shoulder-to-shoulder, and then appears to insert a penny into one girl's ear. He instructs her to tap gently on her ear; the penny magically appears out of her friend's ear. Every year we go to this venue and the girls beg Mark to do that trick. This day, I caught him taking some time out of his lunch hour on a hot day to go see a little shop the girls had set up and were very proud of.*

Kathleen *Mark seems to develop a very special bond with his clinic horses. I knew Buck when Mark was clinicing with him years ago, then Mouse who followed Buck, and now Rocky (shown here) is following Mouse. Mark and his clinic horses often become an inspiration of what can be possible between a person and a horse. With his clinic horse, he can demonstrate how one might influence movement by thinking. He models consistency with his clinic horse and uses him to work with participants' horses if necessary. Rocky came to Mark a little worried and a little bracey, so during clinics, Mark is often working on the same things that his students are. I think that's really helpful for people to see—that Mark's horses don't just magically and instantly become soft and quiet and lovely. Mark has to do the work just like anyone else.*

Patience

ANYONE WHO HAS SPENT ANY TIME AROUND HORSES, and has paid attention to how they do things when they are out in the herd, knows how patient horses can be. For instance, one horse might wait for hours, standing with a foot cocked and its head down, until the more dominant horse standing by the water trough or feed pile moves away. Only then will the first horse slowly make its way over and get a drink or begin eating. If the more dominant horse comes back, the first horse might move back to its original position and once again wait … for as long as it takes.

One of the big keys to working with horses is the ability for the handler to be patient. Generally speaking, horses will learn the specific task we are trying to teach them in exactly the amount of time it takes for them to understand it … no sooner, no later, providing, of course, that we are presenting the information in a way they can understand. It's when we try to force them into learning things faster than they are capable of understanding that things generally begin to go south.

In the job we do, patience is everything, whether with the people we work with, the horses, or simply being patient with the time we have to spend being away from home. In any given month we will spend countless hours on the road getting to the next venue, visiting about this or that, listening to trucker's chatter on the CB, playing the radio or CD player, or just thinking about family and friends, where we are, where we're going, or where we've been. We may have to spend time at a truck stop, waiting for a busy waitress to bring us our food, or wait while the vehicle in front of us pulls away from the pump so we can get fuel. The travel goes as fast as it goes … no faster, no slower. Being a patient traveler is important.

When at a clinic, patience is also very important. Often we will be waiting for a nervous student to explain what is going on between him or her and their horse. We might be waiting for a horse to explain what is going on between him and their owner. We might be waiting for a gracious host to finish preparing breakfast or dinner, so we can either go to work or go to bed. We might be waiting for a horse or rider to understand what we are trying to teach them, or waiting for a horse or owner to teach us. Sometimes, we might just be waiting …

Regardless, it's never so much the waiting we do … but how we do that waiting.

—M.R.

Kathleen *A lot of a clinic horse's job is standing around—or what looks like standing around. A clinic horse might stand around tied to a fence, a trailer, or a tree, and they also stand around under saddle. The thing is, they're not really "standing around," they're waiting patiently to be called on at a moment's notice. Standing around is their work. They're being asked to wait in a certain way, with a certain mindset. They're being asked to wait with a quiet mind, without worry, and without getting in the way of whatever else might be going on. This might seem easy, but I think that it's actually a lot to ask. My clinic horse may need to wait in one place while Mark's clinic horse—his buddy—leaves. There might be things going on around the clinic horse that could upset him or distract him. And all this is happening in a strange place, far from home, where the only consistent thing in that clinic horse's life is, well … the person traveling with him. That's a big responsibility for us.*

If our clinic horse does have trouble with something, it's our job to be patient with him. Clinicing is a tough job for a horse, and there are some situations we might run across only once every few years. There's a constant and delicate dance going on when one is clinicing on a horse, since we must ride the horse wholly while at the same time wholly teaching the student. That's a tall order. But it's what we do for a living.

In this photo, Mark's horse, Rocky, waits patiently while Mark (out of the frame) explains something to a clinic participant. Rocky will be expected to stand right there until he's asked to do something different. The day won't go any faster if our clinic horse is in a hurry—it'll actually seem to take a whole lot longer.

Mark Rocky is a relatively new horse to me. I picked him up at the end of 2006 from my friend, Lloyd Alm, up in Minnesota, on a very cold and windy day. As a result, I didn't get a chance to ride or work with Rocky before I brought him home. Rocky grew up on Lloyd's cow/calf operation and primarily had done that type of work until I got him, so coming into the clinic world was a bit of a shock to his system. Due to the unusually bad weather in Colorado after I got Rocky home, I didn't have much of a chance to work with him before I took him out on the road. As a result, when we began clinicing together, neither one of us really knew anything about one another.

I found, however, that Rocky was a very quick study, and we got along well together almost right from the first ride. In the beginning, Rocky did struggle a little with the idea of standing still for relatively long periods of time, which is a very important part of his new job. But soon enough, he began to pick up on the idea, and by the time this photo was taken, he was able to quietly stand and wait for me without the bother or worry he exhibited only a few weeks earlier, during the first clinic we worked together.

Kathleen *Here is my clinic horse, Jupiter, standing tied to a tree in Florida. This was his first clinic trip, and on this day, his buddy Rocky was resting up due to a swollen eye. So here he is, in a strange place very far from home, without his companion, quietly standing tied to a tree. This is where Jupiter went whenever I didn't need him or when I wanted to give him a rest, and he just stood there until I came to get him again. This kind of behavior has become more and more important to me as I rely on my horses more to help me with my job, and that's why I took this picture. I wanted to give Jupiter credit where credit was due.*

Mark Kathleen bought Jupiter as a resale project in the late fall of 2006. However, after working with him only a short time, she decided to keep him for herself. He is rock steady, easy to get along with, and a perfect gentleman in nearly every situation he is presented with … all extremely important aspects when choosing a horse to travel thousands of miles with over long periods of time. Here he shows one of the most important aspects of the job … patience.

Kathleen *This photo was also taken in Florida, and it shows patience and softness from each of the subjects. Both Mark and Rocky are on the job, and both are very soft and settled, which is something I know Mark practices being better at all the time. This photo, to me, epitomizes the feeling I get when I'm around Mark. To me, Mark exudes a quiet confidence and a belief that everything's going to work out okay, one way or another. That's a really important part of who he is as a person and as a horseman, and that's what I see here.*

Mark Rocky and I are waiting for our next student to come into the arena. I like this photo because it tells a lot about the relationship building between Rocky and me. I am watching as the student is bringing her horse around the arena and to the gate, which is behind me. In the short time Rocky and I have been working together, he has already picked up on the fact that when my focus is on a student, he and I are "on the job" and I may need to call on him at any given time. However, Rocky has also picked up on the fact that a group of yearlings are being fed over in the pasture on the property next door. Still, because my focus is on our student, he keeps one ear on me—just in case I might need him.

Kathleen *I like this picture even more than the previous one, maybe because Mark is looking down and that brings the whole focus in and makes this a portrait of a private, maybe introspective moment. The more I look at this picture, the more I see in it. Waiting never seems to bother Mark, and I can see that waiting is actually a gift in a lot of ways. If we can stay quiet and settled during those periods of waiting, we can see and feel and hear lots of things we would miss if we bulled right through those times. This picture is a portrait of "active inactivity," where both Mark and Rocky are actively waiting, actively patient. Being patient is hard work.*

Mark This photo was taken just a few seconds after the last one. By now it has become clear it will be a few more minutes before the student will be in the arena because she has stopped to chat with a friend. Rocky and I will wait. With my focus now off the student, the ear Rocky had on me just a second before goes over to the yearlings being fed. The softness in his body tells us he hasn't left me, physically or mentally. He is simply occupying his time—just as I am—while together we patiently wait.

Kathleen This is Jupiter again, tied to the arena fence in Georgia during the course of the day. This photo was taken on Jupiter's first day of work with me, and when I saw this kind of behavior from him, I was very pleased. At a clinic, if we need to go do a trailer loading, some round pen work, or go have lunch, our horses might stand like this, unsupervised, for hours at a stretch. That's a lot of patience.

It seems like a lot of what we do in this job is wait—us and the horses both. One of the things we seem to work on when we're traveling and doing clinics is making as few waves as possible. At any given time, it's like we're part of a river that's flowing somewhere. We can choose to be the water, and flow on down to our destination with the rest of the water, or we can be the rock that the water has to go around.

I don't believe I've ever seen Mark hurry. I've seen him make sure something gets done quickly if it needs to, but I've never seen him hurry. Patience is another one of those traits that if we want to bring it to our horsemanship, we're best off practicing it in life and then bringing it to our horsemanship.

Kathleen *We did some work near Las Vegas for a place that gave trail rides to the public, a "dude string," we'd call it. They had almost a hundred horses there, and every day they'd bring up a bunch, saddle them, and tie them to a hitch rail where the horses would wait, sometimes all day, for clients to come—or not come. The horses do this year-round, in the cold of winter and the heat of summer. They're cheerful horses. They understand and like their jobs, and in this photo, that's what I see; these are happy, hardworking horses that bring joy to visitors, and bread and butter to the business that owns them. The morning this photo was taken was bitterly cold. We were working down in a canyon, and the wind could whip through there and just about take your hide off. The sun has just come over the rim of the canyon, and I remember that I hurriedly snapped a couple shots, this among them, then quickly put my camera away so I could put my gloves back on.*

Mark Having worked a number of dude strings over the years, this photo brings back a lot of good memories for me. There was many a cold morning back then when we would saddle the string, tie them to the hitch rail, and wait for someone to come and ride with us. Sometimes folks would show up, other times they wouldn't. Either way, the horses would always patiently stand and wait.

Kathleen and I were doing some work for some good folks who have a dude operation near Las Vegas, Nevada, and she took this photo early one morning while we were waiting for the crew to finish up their morning chores, so we could begin our work with them.

It was unusually cold in Vegas during the time we were there, often in the mid- to lower teens in the morning, and not much warmer during the day. On top of that, the wind would often blow 15 to 30 miles an hour down the canyon we were in, and it generally made for a pretty brisk day. Here, these horses had just been brought out of their pasture, been groomed and saddled, and were now standing quietly at the hitch rail. The chill in the air is evident in this photo, as is the patience these great horses exhibit, even in what for them must be some relatively extreme conditions.

Kathleen *This might just look like a nice picture of Mark's horse Rocky, but it's quite a bit more than that. This is actually Rocky waiting to go to work. On this morning, Mark had gone to check on a clinic participant's horse before coming to get him. The other clinic horse along on this trip had already left the paddock, and Rocky was left in there alone. So there he stood, watching for Mark. He's not worried, he's just looking, he's even got a foot cocked. We spend a lot of time with our horses on the road, and I think between the sheer time we spend and the fact that we're the only consistency for them in that life, we develop a pretty close bond. Horses really like to work with Mark because he's so consistent, and that consistency breeds dependability and trust. Rocky waits patiently, ready to work but not upset by the fact he's all alone and Mark's not there yet. Again, he's on the job and ... waiting.*

One thing I really enjoy seeing in Mark's clinic horses is how they will look for him when he is away from them. If his horse is tied up somewhere, he will turn so he can watch Mark leave and then keep an eye out for him until he returns. They don't get upset that he's gone, they just quietly watch for him. I think that is a nice feeling, to know your horse is looking for you.

Softness

SOFTNESS IS ONE OF THOSE INTANGIBLES IN HORSEMANSHIP—or in life for that matter—that we all try to achieve in one way or another but sometimes struggle to find. Now I am certainly not claiming I know what softness is for everything and everyone on the planet because I don't. I'm also not claiming to have the market cornered on softness because I don't have that either. What I am saying, however, is that it is certainly something we'll never find, if we don't try.

A long time ago I came to understand that, at least for myself, to achieve what I feel is true softness in my horses, I must first be willing to practice that same softness in everything else I do. That means that I'm not just working on softness when I'm working with a horse but also when I'm pushing a wheel barrow, driving down the road, opening a gate, visiting with friends or family, or performing any number of other seemingly mundane tasks one does throughout the day. Unfortunately, I don't always get it right because, as with so many other things in life, it's a work in progress. However, after many years of practice I will say this—I am finally getting the feeling that, at least these days, I may be getting it right more times than I'm not.

In the pages that follow, we get an opportunity to see examples of varying degrees of softness and the effects that softness has—whether it's with the horses we are working with, the tools we use, or even the people who are nearby.

—M.R.

Kathleen *Softness is something that Mark introduced me to many years ago, and is one of the things that I decided to pursue in my horsemanship and in my life. Softness is something that is an ongoing project, as once I achieve what I think at the time is soft, I get a glimpse of another layer of softness underneath. It's become very clear to me that softness isn't something we "do," it's not a technique or a movement. Softness is a way of being. Softness is a choice. I can't say I'm completely comfortable with that choice all the time, but I can say I sure give it a try.*

This photo was taken in Florida, and it is part of a series of photos I took during the interaction Mark and Rocky had with this horse and rider. I kept an eye out for opportunities to take photos of Mark physically interacting with horses and riders because I felt like that was a good way to show who he is. This photo shows the "guiding" part of softness. Softness isn't a lack of direction, or being "limp." Part of softness is the ability to offer guidance, and that's what Mark's doing here. He's not blocking the student's horse from coming over to Rocky, rather he's guiding him to a different place, and that's part of what makes soft "soft."

Mark I feel very strongly that when we practice softness in everything we do, whether with horses or not, it eventually just becomes a *feel* that is second nature … much like our responses are when we drive a vehicle. When we first began driving, for instance, we had to think about every little thing we did—how much pressure to put on the accelerator so the vehicle moved but didn't shoot forward out of control, how much pressure to put on the brake so we would decelerate smoothly and not jerk to a stop, when to let go of the steering wheel coming out of a turn so the vehicle would straighten on its own and not crash into a tree or other vehicle, and so on. Yet through practice these things have all become second nature and we seldom if ever think about them when we drive.

Softness is the same way. The more we practice the more it just becomes the norm, and the more that softness will begin to affect those around us in a positive way. In this photo I've climbed down from Rocky to help a student work with her hands. Rocky is standing next to a horse he's never met, but his mind is quiet and his body is soft, so the new horse isn't an issue for him. The rider's horse, however, a second before this photo was taken, did not necessarily have a quiet mind or soft body. He was a little distracted with Rocky's presence, so he not only ended up forming a thought, *who is that new horse,* but he had also begun to act on that thought, *maybe I should go check him out*—he has turned his head and leaned in Rocky's direction.

Before he could actually take a step, I've reached out and gently placed my hand on his nose, quietly asking him to come off of that thought and replace it with one that might be more beneficial for him and his rider, such as him reestablishing straightness in his body. In response to the hand touching him, his entire body has softened, starting with his ears, then permeating outward in both directions. Here we can see his eyes have slowly closed and his jaw and neck have begun to lose their tightness. Looking closely, one can actually see a number of examples of softness in action in this photo.

Kathleen *One thing we don't really get in the Rocky Mountains where we live is fog, so when I woke up in Florida to thick fog, I was kind of excited about the possibilities it offered. When it's foggy, it's very quiet, especially early in the morning, so as we did our morning chores, I found I wasn't distracted by noises around the farm and I was very aware of the visual effect the fog had on the sights around me. This horse had been turned out in a pasture behind Mark's trailer, and I took a few photos of her. To me, this picture looks quiet as well—there's no noise, just this white horse out there silently eating her breakfast beneath the Spanish moss.*

Mark Whenever I discuss softness in relationship to humans working with horses, the example I always use is the idea of the horse being just as soft when we're on or around them as they are when they are in the field or pasture by themselves. Kathleen took this photo early one morning, right after the sun came up, and the horses that lived at the clinic venue had already been fed. There was a little fog left over from the night before, and this old mare had recently made her way over to the feed.

Everything about her is soft—the way she stands, the way her head and neck reach for the hay, the muscles in her body, and even the look in her eye while she eats. I believe the only way a horse can achieve this kind of softness is by having a quiet and relaxed mind, which this old girl obviously has right now. To me, this is true softness in a horse, and it is the feel and state of mind I try to nurture when I work with them.

Kathleen *I didn't really have any frame of reference for what Mark was talking about when he first mentioned "softness" to me in relation to horsemanship all those years ago. The softness he was talking about was not even visible to me at that point in my horsemanship journey. Since then, I've learned to see and feel softness and to apply it to my everyday life. I loved this photo of Mark and Rocky as soon as I saw it, and now I know why—we've got lots of softness here, both in the subjects and in the photo itself. This photo shows that softness is not a "frame" or a head position. Softness isn't just flexion at the poll or a soft jaw. Softness comes from the inside of the horse and then appears on the outside. Mark and Rocky have a loop in the rein here, yet Rocky is soft throughout his body. That softness is coming from the inside.*

Mark When I first began to ride Rocky, he was a little tighter in both his mind and his body than I really like to feel from my saddle horses. He was also very easily distracted, and in a fairly big hurry most of the time. I think part of the reason Rocky was having so much trouble early on was because up until I bought him, pretty much just one person had ridden him since he was started as a youngster. He had gotten used to that person and the way he rode and worked, and with me riding him, it was just … well … different.

Even though Rocky was struggling with what appeared to be the differences between the way I rode and the way his previous owner rode, I simply kept offering him softness in everything I did with him, from catching to saddling to riding to feeding to whatever. Eventually, he began to find a way to let himself relax a little, and settle into a different way to feel and to go.

This photo was taken after about our twelfth or thirteenth ride together, and if one compares Rocky's look and demeanor to the horse in the previous photo, we can start to see some clear comparisons between a horse that is soft when it is in the pasture by itself, and a horse that is soft with a rider. Again, for me that idea is the ultimate in softness—to be able to achieve the same feel when I'm with my horses that they have when they're on their own.

Kathleen *This picture shows one of the biggest challenges of riding a horse while one is teaching—riding the horse with integrity while teaching with integrity. I struggled a lot with this when I first started working clinics with Mark, and I know I didn't do it very well at first. It was more difficult than I had imagined, this skill of doing two things wholly and well at the same time, and having it work out well for me, my horse, the student, and their horse. But like anything we do, the only way to get better at it was to practice, and practice I did, and still do.*

When I first began working fulltime with Mark, he talked with me quite a bit about the "lineage" of The Work. The Work was passed from Walter Pruitt to Mark, and then from Mark to myself, among others. We talked about how important it is that The Work stay true to the basic philosophies upon which it was founded—that The Work has integrity. That means that we try pretty hard not to take shortcuts, because if we started doing that, pretty soon The Work wouldn't be The Work any more. One of the ways we do that is to ride our clinic horse in a fully present and active manner, no matter what else is going on or how tired we are, or how okay our horse may feel. That's part of the integrity of The Work.

Here, Mark works with Rocky while teaching a student. Mark doesn't just use his clinic horse as a sofa. Mark is fully engaged with his horse while also being fully engaged with his student. It's a gift and a craft he's honed over the years because it's important to him. He is simultaneously offering everything he has to his own horse and to the student and their horse. Softness is what's being offered here, and we can see it in everyone involved in the scene: Mark, Rocky, the student, and her horse. Everyone's soft, and I think that Mark would probably call that a pretty good day's work.

Mark There seems to be a lot of emphasis these days in certain circles of the horse world to sort of hurry a horse's training along; get them walking, trotting, and cantering with a rider on their back almost as soon as they are first started under saddle. While I did get myself sidetracked into that way of thinking and working for a while, it didn't take me all that long to go back to working more along the lines of what I had learned while growing up—that it's better to go slow and be correct than it is to go fast and run the risk of glancing over things.

For me, softness is the foundation for everything else I will ever do with my horse. If I don't have softness, I am missing a huge piece of the horse. In fact, I am probably missing the best piece of the horse—that piece from which everything else comes. Still, in order for that softness to come, he and I must first try to develop a working relationship based on trust. In order for that to happen, I must first be dependable in his eyes, and the only way for me to be dependable is for me to be consistent in everything I do. And part of that consistency is understanding that true softness can't be hurried.

When this photo was taken, Rocky and I had spent close to seventy hours together working on developing softness between us, and we had not yet been out of a walk. Now, it should be said here that with Rocky's background in ranching, I know we could have easily trotted and/or loped if we needed to get a specific job done. Trotting and loping were never an issue. The issue was how the trot and lope would feel.

What Rocky and I have between us in this photo is part of the kind of softness I would like to feel in everything we do from this point forward, no matter what direction, what speed, or what circumstance. From this mental and physical place, everything is possible.

Kathleen *We get good at what we practice, whatever we practice. I've often heard Mark say, "How we practice is how we'll go." Mark practices softness in everything he does, so when it comes to being soft around horses, he can just keep doing what he's been doing all along.*

We can see that here as Mark closes a gate from horseback. Even a gate can be closed softly, using a minimum of muscle, with direction. Mark's hand is open, and although a rider is coming up behind him, he's not in a hurry. This photo of Mark is both practicing being soft and the result of Mark practicing being soft. It's a circle, in a lot of ways, which feeds itself. Each day, we have countless opportunities to make the choice to either practice being soft or practice being not-so-soft, and that choice is up to us. Opening and closing this gate was simply a chance for Mark to practice softness. I bet getting the gate open and then closed was a secondary objective. That change in perspective can sure transform the way we look at getting through our day. Getting through the day can become not so much about what we do, but how we do it.

Mark As I have said, I picked up Rocky in late December of 2006, and didn't really start riding him until January, when I started taking him on the road with me. Many of the photos Kathleen took of us were taken during the first couple of months we worked together, and as such she was actually able to photograph and document a number of "firsts" for us. This photo represents one of those firsts—the first time Rocky and I opened and closed a gate together.

At first, opening and closing a gate horseback doesn't sound like that big a deal, especially for someone who has a horse that understands how to do it. Actually, I'm sure that Rocky had opened and closed gates in the past for his previous owner. But up until this day Rocky and I hadn't had an opportunity to work one together.

As far as I'm concerned, opening a gate isn't necessarily a task to perform, it's simply an opportunity to work on softness. In fact, I feel the work the two of us had done on being soft up to this point allowed this job on this day to be relatively effortless. He was able to move his feet where I needed them to be in order to get in position to open the gate, pass through it, and then close it—which is what is depicted in this photo.

One of the things I have been interested in over the years is the effect a soft touch from a human has on seemingly inanimate objects. To my eye, very often the object that is being touched appears to somehow take on a softer appearance. Here I have reached down to close the gate, which I am offering to do as softly as I can. Even though the gate is made of metal, to my eye it seems as if the metal has been somehow modified to appear more forgiving than it actually is.

Mark I guess I'm a little particular about riding a dirty horse; it's never something I do if I can help it. I suppose that comes from the way I was taught to groom horses as a kid, and even the way we used to groom our horses when I was managing the dude strings later on. Dude string horses have a difficult job as it is. I always believed the least we could do for them was make sure they were clean before they went to work.

The same grooming rituals I began as a kid and carried through to our dude horses, I also use with the horses I ride today. I first use a curry to get the big chunks of dirt off, and then I go over the entire horse with a body brush, making sure the horse is clean and ready for the day. Here, I am actually bent over and currying the underside of Rocky's belly, removing the dirt he had so painstakingly placed there during the night. While bent over, I have laid my left hand, the one holding the body brush, on his back. The hand on his back is more of a soft touch between us than it is anything else … a way for the two of us to get our day going in the right direction before even getting the saddle out.

Like the previous photo of the gate, I feel that this is another example of softness from a human giving an inanimate object—in this case the brush—a little different perspective. To me, a brush sitting off by itself looks different than it does in a hand that is soft.

Kathleen *Working on this project as a photographer was an exercise in softness too. Sometimes I had a specific subject or idea I was looking to shoot, and other times I was just generally keeping an eye out for anything that might be useable. In order to do both things, I had to have a pretty soft focus on what was going on around me. Oftentimes, what I ended up shooting started at the periphery of my vision. If I'd had a hard focus on the visual only right in front of me, I'd have missed what truly needed to be shot. I spent a lot of time just sitting and waiting and watching, patiently. That takes softness, too. Patience is soft. Patience takes a quiet mind. Seeing something as a picture takes a soft and quiet mind.*

Every morning that I was shooting, I hung around the fringes of whatever Mark was doing to prepare for the day. Here, he's getting ready to bridle his horse. Again, it's the incidental details I chose to photograph, and this is usually a pretty mundane moment in a horseman's life. Mark has bridled horses thousands and thousands of times in his life, but we can see that although this task might be commonplace, he's doing it with deliberation and looking for something very specific—softness.

Mark I am a firm believer that if we don't offer the horse softness in everything we do with them, it will be difficult for them to offer softness back in everything they give in return. Again, for me it's about consistency. The more consistent we can be, the more dependable we become, and therefore the more trustworthy we will be to the horse.

I think a horse knows there is an inconsistency when we are trying to teach them to be "soft" when we are riding, yet we are hard as a rock when we do other things. For me, leading, groundwork, grooming, and tacking up are also great places to work on softness between our horses and ourselves. With horses being the subtle animals that they are, I just can't help but believe the little things we do aren't just as important to them, if not more, than the big things we do with them.

Kathleen *Mark offers a clinic format where participants get a chance to do some unmounted exercises every morning. The exercises are designed to help the students put a feel behind certain concepts and theories they might use in their horsemanship, such as softness, centering, intent, and focus. The exercises also tend to be an icebreaker among the students as they interact with each other.*

In this photo, Mark talks with a few students who have just completed an unmounted exercise on being centered. This was the first day of a clinic, and all of these people had just met each other for the first time within the last hour. Some of them had never met Mark before. People can be pretty nervous and excited on the first day of a clinic, and I've seen people so nervous that they had trouble talking or performing simple motor tasks. But here, everyone is soft, relaxed, and attentive. This looks like a good learning environment. A student (horse and human alike) can't learn if he or she is tense, scared, or defensive. I don't think that Mark softened up these students by simply giving them something to do; I think he offered and modeled softness and they were naturally drawn toward, and reassured by, that softness. They, in turn, were able to offer each other softness. As a result, this whole environment, including the people and things in it, are soft.

Kathleen *The following photos are from some work Mark did at a clinic in California with a big Appaloosa that was having trouble leading. He was very distracted, and his owner was having a difficult time asking him to not run her over. Mark worked with him for a short period of time, and the five photographs in this series document that work.*

In the first photo, Mark is asking the Appy to not run him over. Mark is soft here, even though he's asking this horse to back off. His face is calm, and there's no emotion in the request. He's simply teaching this horse in a businesslike way what his boundary is. Mark's hands are open on the rope. We can see that although Mark is offering this horse softness, the horse's response is not yet soft.

In the second photo of the series, Mark is talking with the owner while still working with the horse. The horse is outside of Mark's boundary and is staying there, though he's still a little tight. It looks to me like he's got some of his attention on Mark and some on his surroundings. If you compare this photo to the first, Mark doesn't look much different except that he's standing still. His face is calm, his body soft, and his hands are open on the rope.

In the third photo, Mark is asking the horse to back off again. We can see the horse is thinking "backwards" and there's some energy in the rope. Just like the other photos, although Mark is asking this horse to back off, he's doing so softly. He's offering softness, even though this horse cannot yet return it. It was not long after this photo was taken that the Appy began to offer Mark some softness back.

The last two photos, though they don't show the Appy, show some softness coming from the Appy's end of the rope back to Mark. Again, nothing's changed on Mark's part. Now, the feel that's going to the horse from Mark and the feel coming from the horse to Mark are more similar, and we can see that in the rope.

This is the kind of consistency in behavior and presentation that can help us become a positive presence in a horse's life. Because Mark focuses on the pursuit of softness, it creates a consistency in what he does. That consistency is what Mark, and any horse he works with, can hang their hat on—day in and day out.

Mark In this series of photos, I am working with a pretty big horse that is distracted and worried. He was jumping around some, calling to one of his buddies back at the barn, and nearly running over his owner. His owner was having some trouble handling him while he was in that state of mind, so I asked if I could step in. In the first photo, I am simply establishing boundaries, which for me is an arm's-length distance between the horse and myself. I am also working on establishing myself as a presence, something he should at least try to be aware of, even if he's troubled. If he is aware of my presence, he will be a little less likely to run me over accidentally while he's in that distracted state of mind.

This is often a delicate balance between using enough energy to cause the horse to respond in the proper manner, or sending him even further into a more troubled state of mind. Because of that delicate balance, it is imperative that we remain soft and nonjudgmental as to the horse's current behavior, so we can direct him to the desired behavior and state of mind.

In the second photo, the horse has relaxed a little, stopped his feet, and has brought his attention back in the pen long enough for me to visit with his owner about what I am doing and why. Shortly after this photo was taken, the big gelding once again began to get troubled and started moving around and calling to his friend.

He began moving in my direction and stepped inside the boundaries we had just established. In the third photo, I am reestablishing those boundaries using my body movement and energy. Again, I am not upset or angry with him, I'm simply asking him to give me a little room while he's in that state of mind. In that photo, he is mentally coming back to me quicker, and trying to calm his mind. It is important to note here that I am not trying to stop the behavior the gelding is offering, even though it isn't necessarily the behavior we are looking for. I am simply redirecting the energy of the behavior to a little more mutually beneficial place for both of us.

The next two photos, while only showing images of my hands on the rope, tell an interesting little story. The gelding has stepped back and calmed down. He has dropped his head and become a little bit more aware of his immediate surroundings, as opposed to looking back to the barn and calling to his friend. Having softly given him some boundaries and guidelines as to how to act in the situation he is in, he is beginning to gain some confidence in his situation, and in the person handling him. Looking at the rope, we can see the softness the gelding is offering back, even though he isn't in the picture.

167

Tim & Tico

168

I MET TIM HARVEY AND HIS HORSE TICO for the first time in the fall of 2006 when Kathleen and I traveled to his place in Rhode Island to give a clinic. It was clear almost from the start that Tim and I seemed destined to become good friends. During the normal conversations one has when spending time with a clinic host, Tim and I (not surprisingly) found we had similar ideas and ideals when it came to horses and horsemanship, as well as similar interests in other areas, such as martial arts and even the types of trucks we drove. As time went on and our conversations continued, we also found very eerie similarities in our respective childhoods, backgrounds, and life experiences. Many of these similarities were so striking it was almost as if Tim and I had been long lost brothers separated at birth.

The day after we arrived at Tim's place, he took me out to a large pen set back from all the other buildings, pens, and corrals on the place. It was there that he introduced me to his horse, Tico, for the first time. Tico was a six-year-old BLM Mustang that Tim had used as a stallion until only recently, when he had decided to geld him and begin his training. I had seen and worked with a great number of Mustangs over the years, and when Tim mentioned that he hoped I would be able to help him with the progression of Tico's training, I assumed Tico would be "just another Mustang." What I mean by that is that he would look relatively rangy and carry with him the normal Mustang mentality, behaviors, and mindset. In other words, lots of try, but extremely strong on self-preservation, bringing with it all that entails.

As we rounded the corner to Tico's pen and I saw him for the first time, I immediately knew this was not just another Mustang. It was clear there was something very special about this horse, and about the relationship between him and Tim.

At the time, Tim's concern with Tico was how troubled he was whenever Tim would go to catch him. It wasn't that Tim couldn't catch the Mustang, because he could. Rather, it was that Tico couldn't seem to be caught on Tim's terms, or when Tim needed to catch him. He would have to wait until Tico was ready and willing to give Tim permission to approach before he would allow himself to be caught.

Over the next four days of the clinic, I helped Tim teach Tico how to accept the idea of being approached and caught on someone else's terms, while at the same time keeping Tico's character and extremely strong spirit intact. Slowly, Tico began to accept the idea, and over time began to settle into the belief that not everybody who approached him had bad intentions in mind. After that first clinic, I gave the two of them some homework to work on until the next time we would meet, not knowing for sure when that would be.

The photos that follow come from our second meeting, four months after the first. Tim brought Tico sixteen hundred miles from New England to Florida in the middle of the winter, where Kathleen and I were giving a series of three, three-day clinics. Tim signed up for all three clinics, and worked tirelessly every day in an effort to help Tico advance through the remaining struggles he was having ... a true tribute to the dedication and commitment this man has for this wonderful horse.

For me these photos represent a glimpse into the relationship between Tim, Tico, and myself, and the struggles and triumphs we all might have to go through to develop a lasting relationship based on faith, hope, and trust.

—M.R.

Kathleen *When I first began shooting these photos of Tim and Tico, my intent was to take some photos to give to Tim as a gift. So every afternoon that I could, I took my camera to the round pen to see what I could shoot. What I saw on those afternoons and wanted to capture was the truly special bond between this man and this horse. In the end, I think these photos captured much more than that. For many reasons, most known only to themselves, Tim's and Tico's futures are tied inextricably together. Tim may be just a man and Tico may be just a horse, but together they represent hope and redemption. These photos depict more than just horse training—they're a document of what happened between Tim and Tico and Mark. That's a pretty big deal to me because what I wanted to document was something that I wondered if I, or anyone for that matter, could catch in still photographs.*

Mark and I have talked a lot about having the horse's best interest at heart when working with them, and that's what I see here. There's empathy and kindness in both Mark and Tim, even though Tico cannot yet see those things in the two men. But if I had to take a picture of what it means to have a horse's best interest at heart, I think this would be it.

Mark In this photo, the compassion Tim has for his horse is clearly evident in Tim's facial expression and body language. Just as evident is the anxiety Tico shows. Out of fear, the muscles in Tico's chest, neck, and face are tight, he is leaning slightly away from us, his head is high, and he is ready to leave at any moment—yet even as fearful as he is, he remained there, and allowed himself to be touched.

Only four months earlier, when I met Tico for the first time, not only was he nearly impossible to catch, but even when you did catch him, he still didn't want anyone touching him. The fact that on this day Tico stood (even if reluctantly) and allowed a stranger to touch him, while at the same time being approached by a second human, is a real testament to the time and effort both Tim and Tico had put into their relationship since the last time I saw them.

To me, this photo represents the three of us—Tim, Tico, and myself—all standing on the edge of a path on which we were all about to embark. We didn't know how far we would be able to go in the nine days we would be spending together, or even in which direction it would take us. All we knew at this moment was that we were about to take our first step.

Kathleen *This photo was taken at the end of a tough session between Mark and Tico. They've ended in a good place, but they paid a price to get there. That session was tough for me to watch. When I reviewed my photos later, I found a few from the beginning of the session and a few from the end (this one among those), but I had no photos of the hour and a half of work in between. I just couldn't shoot it. I think there was something kind of sacred about that part of Tico's struggle that day, and what Mark did to help him. I feel that if I'd photographed and documented it, I would have violated some secret agreement between Mark and that horse. What I did want to photograph was the result of the session, which to me was a man and a horse who had both given their best to each other, regardless of the cost to themselves. I like that, in this picture, Tico is reaching toward Mark, because that was very hard for him to do at that time. The lead rope is slack and Mark's hand is open on the rope. Between them, they've come through shadows, and there's hope that perhaps Tico, Mark, and Tim can move on from here.*

Mark Working with most troubled horses is a lot like peeling an onion. Once you get past one layer, there is another one right underneath—and sometimes that layer is even stronger than the last. Working with Tico was the epitome of this analogy. While Tim and Tico had made great strides over the past four months, it was clear that Tico was still holding on very strongly to his self-preservation instinct, a fact that would certainly hinder any future training or work between the two of them. Very often, the only way to address a big issue with a troubled horse is to start by looking at what appears to be a smaller issue. On this day, that is what we attempted to do.

One of Tico's issues was that when he became worried or troubled, he would turn and face his handler, head high in the air, eyes wide in a semi-panic, standing with every muscle tight and at the ready just in case he needed to flee. After standing in this position for a few seconds, he would then begin to back away from the handler. Of course eventually he would stop, sometimes on his own, sometimes with help from the handler. But he always maintained this head-high, body-tight defensive position.

We decided before we could go any further in his training, we needed to address this issue. As a result, after Tico had offered this same behavior several times without fail and without change, I began the process of trying to help him come to a softer place, mentally. After the fourth or fifth time that he moved backward in this manner, I simply began to move with him, not trying to force him to continue to move backward, and not asking him to stop, either … just moving with him. Initially, his head got higher, his anxiety level increased dramatically, and his flight instinct kicked in. Still I moved with him. He sped up in his high-headed, backward motion and offered sideways to the right, then sideways to the left. Still I moved with him. He snorted and tried to charge off. I maintained my movement. This went on for what seemed like an eternity, until finally, he offered an ever so slight softening and lowering of his head. At that point, I stopped moving.

Again he started his backward options. Again I moved with him. Eventually he offered the slight lowering of his head, and again I stopped moving. Forty-five minutes later, and after countless repetitions of this action, Tico and I finally came out the other side together. He was no longer panicking and backing away, and he had finally begun to understand it was okay to lower his head and relax when people were around.

This was a very difficult session for me because I hate to have a horse feel as bad as Tico obviously did while we were working. Yet leaving him the way he was wasn't going to help either Tico or Tim, and we had to start somewhere. I tell folks all the time that the training we do today isn't for today … it's for tomorrow. When Kathleen snapped this photo, we had yet to see what tomorrow might bring. But for now, Tico and I were both feeling a little better about the door we had just passed through.

Kathleen *This photo and the one that follows were taken the day after Tico was introduced to ground-driving. For those who don't know, ground-driving (also known as long lining) consists of teaching a horse to stop, turn, and back up using two long lines while standing on the ground, rather than from on his back. Mark usually ground-drives horses as part of his starting process so that the cues for turn, stop, and back up are instilled before the horse is ever saddled. I have to say that Tico was about the most troubled horse I've seen when it comes to ground-driving. While he was pretty troubled about the whole process, in particular he just couldn't bring himself to turn left that first day. Among those who were watching, you could just feel us all rooting, "Just turn left, just turn left, it's right there." What caught my attention that first day, and what we can see here in the photos taken on the second day, is how Mark never changed. He was never in a hurry, he never got emotional, he just consistently asked for the same thing, the same way, over and over. There were times when Tico speeded up, and then Mark went with him, but there was no emotion shown when that happened either. If you look at this photo and the one that follows, you'll see that Mark looks basically the same in both photos, though Tico is offering two different things. Mark's hands, especially, are almost exactly the same in both photos, soft and open yet clearly guiding.*

Mark Tim and Tico had signed up for a series of three, three-day clinics, with a day off after the second three-day clinic. This picture was taken after the second three-day clinic, on our day off. Until now, Tim had done a tremendous amount of ground work with Tico, which included getting him used to ropes around his body and his hind legs. The first four days we worked with Tico, he did really well with everything we asked him to do, once he overcame his initial worry and apprehension. Having all of the other pieces in place, including lunging Tico on a line, we decided on the fifth day to progress to ground-driving. Because he had done so well with everything else, it did surprise me a little that Tico's first reaction to having two lines around him was sheer panic. However, after a relatively short period of time, he seemed to settle in to a point where we could start working on turning. He would readily turn to the right, even though it was pretty quick and reactive. Still, any time I would ask him to turn to the left, he would begin the turn, get just a short way, and then explode back to the right in what appeared to be unbridled terror. We had actually noticed this problem earlier when we were leading him—if something worried Tico, he would turn around to the right and face his handler—very seldom would he do this to the left. We spent the majority of that session helping Tico find a way to quietly turn to the left. At one point, he was able to get just over three-quarters of the left-hand turn completed, before having to spin back to the right.

I couldn't help but make a correlation between what Tico felt he had to do to keep himself from doing this left-hand turn and what some people do to prevent themselves from making some change in their lives. A lot of people will start to change something in their life, and they'll get about three-quarters of the way through that change, and then suddenly feel the need to turn around and run as fast as they can back to what they were doing before, never letting the change become complete. With Tico, I just quietly encouraged him, no matter how troubled or explosive he got, to go to the left … and eventually he did. This picture was taken one day later, and some of the apprehension is still evident. Though he has one ear on me, there is tension on the line around his body on the left side, and his left ear is forward—perhaps looking for a way out.

Mark This photo was snapped just a few seconds after the previous one. Tico has softened his body and begun his left-hand turn, the direction that seemed nearly impossible for him just a day earlier. I believe this photo actually documents the moment at which Tico began to believe that we were trying to help him understand there would be more to life than simply standing in his pen all day, day in and day out.

Until this moment, Tico has relied completely on himself for all the decisions that were made in his life. At this moment, he is exploring the possibility of allowing himself to accept helpful direction from someone else.

In the previous photo, Tico had one ear on me, and one ear forward, perhaps looking for a way out if he should feel the need to leave the situation. Here, he has begun to soften to his left-hand turn, with one ear on me and one ear on the cotton line that is supplying the request. In the past, he has always turned to the right to face the human that was handling him whenever he felt he was in trouble. While obviously keeping track of me on his right, he is also exploring the possibility that maybe … just maybe … he might also be able to turn the other way, too, when asked to do so. That's a big step for a horse that, up till now, has only known how to rely on his instincts to keep him "safe."

Kathleen *Photography is interesting to me because through it we can document a moment in time—a split-second that will never happen again, ever. And by taking a picture that moment can appear again, even though often times the image is a shell of the moment that passed—it has no life inside it. A photo can't capture the sound of the birds calling in the background, or the warm smell of the horse at the other end of the lens. This scene just appeared before me one day as Tim and Tico worked together, a lucky accident of appropriate angles and light. I think this picture is more than a shell, because even though Tim's back is to the camera, we know that something is passing between him and his horse. Only they know exactly what it was, and that's okay. To step in this close to them is enough.*

Mark There is just something about the eye of a troubled horse that shows he is looking for a way to feel better. If you look carefully, you can see an almost complete gamut of emotions emanating from the eye. There's apprehension, worry, nervousness, and doubt. Yet at the very same time, in the very same eye, there is also a hint of trust, faith, commitment, and dedication to the hope that everything is going to work out.

When I first saw this photo of Tico's eye, I felt Kathleen had captured the true essence of this great horse. I still feel that way today.

Mark This photo was taken near the end of our second day with Tico. It's clear he's beginning to feel better about the things we are asking of him—particularly accepting ropes around his body. Interestingly enough, later in the day after our session was over, Tim noticed that—for the first time ever— Tico was hanging his head out his stall door and looking around. Up until this point, Tico would hang out in the back of his stall, and pretty much ignore the people that passed by. Tim was further surprised when Tico allowed Tim to go up and pet and scratch him while he was looking out the door … something that was next to impossible just one day earlier.

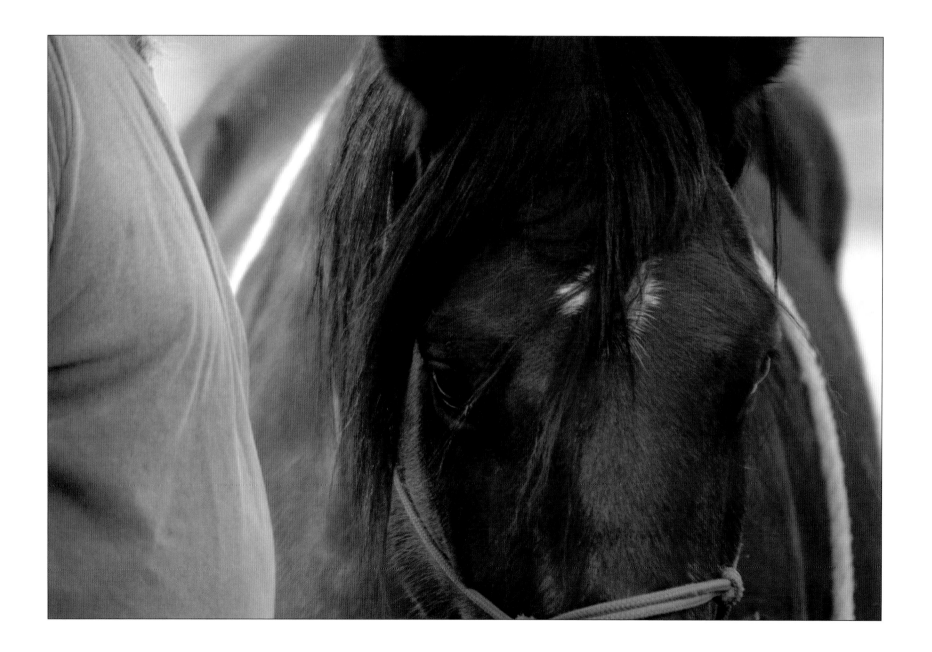

Kathleen *It wasn't until I reviewed all the photos of Tico that I noticed something that's very evident in this photo, which is how big Tico looks in the photos taken earlier on in the clinics. Tico is about 14.2 hands in real life, but in this photo he looks huge, even next to Mark, who's about six feet tall. In looking back through the pictures, it almost looked like Tico could puff himself up to appear nearly twice his actual size when he was worried about something. What's surprising is that on film he looks even bigger! If you look at the next photo, Tico looks more his actual size next to Tim, and that photo was taken when he was feeling better about things. I think Tico still has plenty of presence at his "normal" size, he just doesn't have the hard edge he had on him when he appeared bigger and was troubled.*

Mark One of the things I truly regret about my job is that there are times when, no matter how hard we try, some horses are going to get troubled about the things we are asking them to do. Generally, as I did in Tim and Tico's case, I will try to help a horse get through about 80 percent of the trouble they are having, then I will give the horse back to the owner so they can help it the rest of the way. It's great to see the interaction between the owner and horse when they come through that other 20 percent, and the horse lets go of the trouble it was feeling. The only down side for me is that, often, there was still that little bit of trouble the horse was feeling about me when I gave it back to the owner, and as a result, the horse and I almost never get a chance to resolve that little bit of difference that may have been going on between us. Obviously, the most important part of the job is making sure the owner and horse go away feeling good together, because ultimately the relationship is theirs. Because of that, I believe it is extremely important that any big change that is going to happen with a horse needs to take place when the owner is working with it. But still, it is never easy to know that oftentimes I have to leave a horse with that little bit of question in their mind—about that guy they met in that pen that day.

Kathleen   *When Tim and Mark met in the fall of 2006, somehow I knew they would hit it off as friends, as well as be successful as teacher and student. I could just tell. Sometimes it can be awkward to be someone's teacher as well as their friend, but Mark seems to be one of those rare people who can do that well. That's a special gift because I think it would be very difficult for Mark and Tim if they would have to choose between a teacher/student relationship or a friendship. I wanted to take some photos of Mark and Tim working together with Tico, in hopes that I could capture the very special three-way bond between them. This is one of those lucky shots that ended up saying a bit more than I thought it would.*

Mark   This is one of my favorite photos of Tim, Tico, and myself. It was taken toward the end of one of our sessions. Clearly, Tim and Tico are both in a good place with the work they are doing. I have been the teacher up to this point, initiating and directing the work, but always allowing Tim to finish it. Here, with Tim and Tico feeling good about the time they have just spent together, I am still in the picture, but just slightly out of focus. Metaphorically, for me it is a sign of the way things should be. As the student becomes more confident in his knowledge and experience, the teacher begins to fade somewhat into the background, which will, in turn, allow for the student to one day become the teacher.